Global Financial Turbulence in the Euro Area

STUDIES IN POLITICS, SECURITY AND SOCIETY

Edited by Stanisław Sulowski

Institute of Political Science of the University of Warsaw

VOLUME 3

PETER LANG
EDITION

Alojzy Z. Nowak (ed.)

Global Financial Turbulence in the Euro Area

Polish Perspective

PETER LANG
EDITION

Bibliographic Information published by the Deutsche Nationalbibliothek
The Deutsche Nationalbibliothek lists this publication in the Deutsche Nationalbibliografie; detailed bibliographic data is available in the internet at http://dnb.d-nb.de.

Reviewer: Professor Andrzej Stępniak, University of Gdańsk

This publication was financially supported by
the Faculty of Management of the University of Warsaw.

ISSN 2199-028X
ISBN 978-3-631-66565-7 (Print)
E-ISBN 978-3-653-05960-1 (E-Book)
DOI 10.3726/978-3-653-05960-1

Peter Lang Edition is an Imprint of Peter Lang GmbH.

Peter Lang – Frankfurt am Main · Bern · Bruxelles · New York ·
Oxford · Warszawa · Wien

This publication has been peer reviewed.

www.peterlang.com

Contents

About the Contributors

Authors and Editors

Alojzy Z. Nowak, Professor, Vice-Rector of The University of Warsaw, former Dean of The Faculty of Management, University of Warsaw, from 2005 until 2012.

Kazimierz Ryć, Professor of Faculty of Management, University of Warsaw, former Dean of Faculty of Management, The University of Warsaw from 1999 until 2005.

Yochanan Shachmurove, Professor of Economics and Business, The City College, The Graduate School and University Centre of the City University of New York.

Patrick O'Sullivan, Ph.D., Grenoble Ecole de Management, Visiting Professor at University of Warsaw, patrick.osullivan@grenoble-em.com.

Grzegorz Tchorek, Ph.D., The Faculty of Management, University of Warsaw, National Bank of Poland.

Part I

Alojzy Z. Nowak

Globalisation as a Macroeconomic Megatrend

Introduction

The process of globalisation really started with great geographical discoveries, which in many cases led to colonisation of the newly found territories. There is no doubt, however, that the dynamics of supra-national relationships of an economic nature received a violent thrust together with the quick growth of the capitalist system. The market as the key element of the system increasingly forced efforts aiming at abolition of all sorts of regulation and trade barriers.

Historical Stages Upon the Way to Globalisation of Economy

In international circulation, countries began to make use of their relative advantages stemming from geographic conditions, natural and human resources as well as military power. Adam Smith, a Scottish thinker and the author of free market theory, assumed three principal measures of value in his work *An Inquiry into the Nature and Causes of the Wealth of Nations*, namely: precious metals (including gold and silver), cereals, and human labour. At that time, indeed, these formed the basis for general considerations of utility and exchangeable value in any commercial and trade activities.

Another stage of globalisation can be found in great discoveries made throughout the 19th century and, more broadly, with the industrial revolution and further growth of capitalism. Actually, it was quite early into the century that David Ricardo published, in 1817, his book *The Principles of Political Economy and Taxation*, being the first author to have proposed a concept of comparative costs which has become the basis of the theory of international trade exchange prevalent until our days. The essence of it comes down to explanation of the mechanism of mutually advantageous international exchange of goods and services in a situation of goods manufacturing costs being considerably lower in one than in another party to the relationship. The occurrence of relative differences in costs of production, measured with labour input is an important premise for development of specialisation and international trade. That theory, well proven in practice, gave an enormous impulse to international trade exchange.

The most informed analysis of capitalist development of the day in the early 20th century, as well as the consequences for global economy was presented by

John Maynard Keynes in the 1930s. The Great Depression on 1930s in the USA, which quickly spread into a devastating worldwide economic and social crisis, also causing a real decline in the world trade, was the most spectacular example of inadequacy of most previous theories about self-regulating markets. The trust in the classical liberal economic system was undermined.

In his most famous work, *The General Theory of Employment, Interest and Money*, published in 1936, the British economist argued that it's not in the nature of the economy to overcome crises on its own. Accordingly, it should be up to state governments to act as crucial market regulators since stimulation of the economy can happen through increased state expenditure, including work done in the public sector, infrastructural investment projects, as well as through enlivened social consumption. Over time, these recommendations, based upon the concept of state intervention have become the foundation of both practice and economic policy of many governments until it is really and today they form an important element of macroeconomic theory.

The influence of Keynes' theory upon the operation of the economy was also quite pronounced in the area of establishment of the new global deal with respect to international economic relationships. Despite his serious illness – a stroke suffered in 1937 – Keynes played a crucial role during the Bretton Woods conference in 1944 where, following years of exchange rate wars and omnipresent state protectionism of the WW2 period, a new monetary deal was established. A system of fixed exchange rates pegging individual currencies to the US Dollar was introduced and its parity exchangeable to gold was specified. This way, the system of fixed exchange rates of individual currencies was anchored in gold via the US Dollar.

The Bretton Woods system allowed for agreed changes of exchange rates of individual currencies in cases where a given country was experiencing permanent external imbalance. In such case currency devaluation could make the adaptation process, agreed with the International Monetary Fund, easier and less severe for the society. The new system relating currency with gold was soon named socially rooted liberalism and with the US Dollar acting as agent in maintaining the relationship with gold – a sort of benevolent tyranny had emerged in respect of exchange rates.

The Bretton Woods system performed well for many years in practical terms, however it was rather costly in political terms. Devaluation which made it easier to implement the program of adaptation to ever-changing market conditions was politically risky for governments because it required a great deal of social sacrifice. Anyway, the system worked because its alternative – a system of floating exchange rates – seemed even worse; it had been rejected after the WW2 in the wake of bad experiences with competitive devaluations and instability in the 1930s.

However, turbulence faced by the global economy in 1970s contributed to dissolution of the Bretton Woods system and resulted in gradual return of floating exchange rates. A system of floating exchange rates combined with the inflation target policy run by central banks should – in theory – ensure efficient operation of markets, but failed to do so in reality. Neither were currencies' exchange rates reflecting the so-called economic fundamentals nor was the achievement of the inflationary target ensuring proper balance in the economy.

At the same time, 1960s and the later years of the 20th Century have been a period of a great offensive by proponents of monetarist economics. Its most prominent exponent, Professor Milton Friedman (awarded with Nobel Prize in economics) challenged Keynes's theory and argued that inflation directly depends on the size of money supply in an economy and that inadequate monetary policy, in the long run, always seems to lead to either price inflation or deflation rather than to changes in the level of production, so – contrary to s the assertions of Keynes' advocates – policies of economic stimulation by the government (at least when associated with monetary expansion), resulting in higher inflation, and fails to bring a permanent reduction of unemployment. Accordingly, state intervention policy, instead of supporting commercial entities operating in the market, actually hinders them and acts as barrier to greater dynamics of commercial exchange between individual countries, thus disturbing the very foundations of healthy competition among them. Therefore, it is only free market – as previously maintained by Adam Smith – that provides favourable conditions to solve global economic problems.

Under conditions of increasing globalisation and global economy financialisation, largely resulting from the dominance of the monetarist theory, the inefficiency of the floating rates system was also becoming a barrier to trade relationships and economic cooperation. That latter hindrance was experienced more and more seriously by the European Union as it found floating currency exchange rates a barrier to further EU integration. This became an imperative reason to renounce national currencies and establish the common currency in the form of Euro.

The founding of the customs union in 1958 had, historically, considerable importance on the road toward elimination of many economic barriers. The free trade zone in which no internal customs duties applied was supplemented by the common external tariff adopted by its member states. Then since 1987 (single Europe Act) all the trade occurring within the European Community since has taken place in a genuinely single market with no inner borders of any kind.

That stage also stimulated development of integration processes in the EEC's institutional layer. Finally, it was becoming more and more evident that the dynamics of economic integration inevitably leads not only to the establishment of the single internal market, including free movement of goods, services, persons and capital, but to deepened monetary cooperation as well. This was also a requirement of increasingly intense dynamic process of increasing global trade, investment and interdependence known as globalisation.

The need for a new quality in monetary integration of the European Union member states, therefore, led straight to another important event in the history of European integration, namely to the Treaty of Maastricht of 1992. It was to carry on and creatively implement plans and assumptions proposed by earlier visionaries and, indeed, true father of today's European Union, such as Robert Schuman, Jean Monnet, Konrad Adenauer, Alcide De Gasperi, Paul-Henri Spaak and Altiero Spinelli.

The Euro as the common currency was introduced on 1 January 1999, initially in the form of non-cash transactions and on 1 January 2002 it was extended to cash form as well in 12 EU member states. Many countries included in the Euro Area featured very divergent levels of economic development, macroeconomic situation and political stability – on the one hand there was Germany, France, Netherlands or Luxembourg while on the other hand Italy, Portugal or, later on, Greece.

Admittedly, the European Union's common currency area was preceded by the requirement that the participating countries should first attain the Maastricht Treaty Convergence criteria.

Among them, monetary and fiscal criteria were most important. Monetary ones included as follows:

- The price stability criterion (relating to inflation) – specified an admissible limit of inflation rate. The annual rate of inflation over a period of one year before the moment of inspection was not allowed to exceed 1.5 percentage point of the average level of inflation in three member states recording the lowest inflation rate. It was agreed that inflation would be measured using comparable indices of consumer prices and cover a period of one year directly precedent to the moment individual countries are qualified to monetary union.
- The interest rate criterion required that over a period of one year before the moment of inspection, an average long-term percentage rate was not in excess of 2 percentage points of the average of similar interest rates in three European Union member states recording the lowest inflation rate.
- The exchange rate criterion related to the currency of a country-candidate to become EU member. Such a state had to participate, for the minimum period

of two years, in the European Exchange Rate Mechanism (ERM II) and limits of exchange rate oscillations were set at +/- 2.25%. A couple of years later, however, the range was extended to +/-15%.

Fiscal criteria, on the other hand, related to the following:

- At the moment of inspection, the maximum admissible level of aggregate public debt was specified at 60% GDP.
- At the moment of inspection the allowable level of budgetary deficit with respect to gross domestic product was set at 3% over a year.

At present, following many years of experience in the Euro Area operation, it can in retrospect be said that from the very outset that countries participating therein mostly failed to satisfy the above-mentioned fiscal and monetary criteria. In fact, decisions on membership of individual countries in the Euro Area were largely political. The global financial crisis at the end of the first decade of the 21st Century has also exposed a number of problems in the way Euro Area operates, both in terms of fiscal and institutional affairs. While from the point of view, interesting in the present context, of the evolution of economic globalisation, the Euro Area as the whole plays a significant role, its very future and nature have become an object of a great deal of dispute among politicians and scholars. The effectiveness of reforms planned in Euro Area is going to depend on the member states' will actually to implement them and then to comply thereto. However, it is quite hard to force countries to respect common arrangements if they don't really perceive stability and competitiveness of Euro Area and the entire European Union as their common good and the object of their common concern and if the institutional system leaves so much room to prioritise national interests over shared common interests.

Global Dilemmas of the 21st Century

A question that should be asked in this context is about the nature of globalisation at the beginning of the 21st Century. Definitions of this notion tend to differ depending on scopes of specialisation of the expert involved. Sociologists define it in a different way than representatives of political science and economists put forth yet another point of view. Let us now adopt diversified definitions seen in the literature, following John Ravenhill (2005).[1] Globalisation can be defined as:

1 Ravenhill J., *Global Political Economy*, Oxford: Oxford University Press, 2005.

1. Intensification of social relations on the global scale (A. Giddens),
2. Integration of the global economy (R. Gilpin),
3. De-territorialisation; or a growth of supranational interpersonal relations (J. A. Scholte),
4. Global economy in which national economies – and therefore also national economic and management strategies – largely lose their importance (P. Hirst, G. Thompson).

Today, these general definitions describing the notion of globalisation no longer seem sufficient, in particular in relation to such areas as modern concepts of organisation, management, the impact of impressive progress in cutting edge technologies upon market functioning on the global scale, effects of megatrends in the global economy on market operation in the long run, including, in particular, operation of financial markets.[2]

However, the questions globalisation confronts us with are, at the same time, of more universal nature as they concern such fundamental issues as the following:[3]

- The role of the (nation) State in the (global) economy and the 21st Century society model,
- The values and goals that keep societies together and integrate communities.

These latter crucial values, in turn, are based on a selection of political solutions, which, among other things, relate to the following:

- The sense of justice (lower or higher social stratification),
- Life style, dilemmas regarding all sorts of minorities (ethnic, gender-related phenomena, etc.),
- Sovereignty of individuals, nations, and states.

> *This is also about a consciousness level, because an answer to the question where and how far has globalisation already reached partially depends on what is expected the reform. Visions of globalisation clearly contribute to describe its reality since globalisation is partly structured according to visions, becoming a resultant of confronting forces of "fate" and "choice," while on its own it is neither pure fate, determined with factors beyond our control, nor pure choice resulting from decisions we make.*[4]

---

2 Nowak A.Z., "Współczesny świat w erze turbulencji" (Contemporary World at the Time of Turbulence), in: *Zarządzanie: tradycja i nowoczesność* (*Management: Tradition and Modernity*), Bogdanienko J., Piotrowski W. (eds), Warsaw: PWE, 2013.

3 *ibid.*

4 Morawski W. (2004), "Mapy drogowe globalizacji: Propozycje analityczno- teoretyczne" (Globalisation Road Maps), in: *Wyzwania globalizacji. Odpowiedzi przedsiębiorstw*

In terms of choice in the process of globalisation, there is a number of questions and dilemmas, if only those concerning the model and limits of modernisation. It might be assumed that modernisation still provides us with the following opportunities:[5]

- To raise the levels of welfare of individuals and nations,
- To consolidate prestige and status of the State, of local communities and of family,
- To promote and enrich spiritual and intellectual values.

Apparently, however, these opportunities are perceived and interpreted in different ways, due to fundamental economic and cultural divergences from one nation and country to another. That's why attempts to extend or sometimes to impose a system of values and attitudes pertinent to the Western world, such as consumerism, faith in self-regulatory, positive market effect or human rights provoked criticism and in many cases plain rejection of the modernisation model adopted in the principal actors of global markets, such as the USA or European states.

It might be argued, then, that the following parts of the world found themselves beyond the mainstream, or at least in some sort of opposition to the prevailing model of modernisation:[6]

- The Islamic world, which takes limited benefits from the global economy, but distinctly pronounces its cultural difference. Using the enormous resources of financial capital it has collected (saved) it reinforces real global economic processes, but at the same time it may become a factor potentially destabilising the world in both economic and political terms.
- The underdeveloped world of, mainly in Africa, largely excluded from the benefits and advantages the processes of globalisation bring.
- The world of Chinese civilisation. The specificity of continental China and other Asian countries under an evident cultural influence of China consists in the fact they all are now numbered among the biggest beneficiaries of globalisation while at the same time they retain – which mostly relates to China – quite a separate pattern of development. Actually, what we have here – it seems – is an example of successful (in economic terms) anti-liberal modernisation, i.e. of a model based,

---

(*Globalization Challenges. Entrepreneurs' Replies*), I. Koładkiewicz, W. Kozioł (eds.), Warsaw: University of Warsaw School of Management Press.

5 Nowak A.Z., "Współczesny świat w erze turbulencji" (Contemporary World at the Time of Turbulence).

6 *ibid.*

inter alia, upon a cultural heritage originating from the philosophy of Confucius much more than on well proven patterns derived from the experience of highly-developed Western states.

The achievements of China, on the one hand, contrasted with the most serious post-WW2 financial crisis in the West with its ultraliberal background, on the other hand, prompt many economists and political scientists to far-reaching – although not entirely futurological – conclusion that we are nowadays witnessing the twilight of Western civilisation dominance.[7]

Joseph E. Stiglitz, awarded the Nobel Prize in economics, goes even further in saying that the global economic crisis, largely caused by behaviour of America, has brought more detriment to the fundamental values of the world of Western civilisation and its economy than any totalitarian system.[8]

However, according to a number of experts, the essence of Western civilisation's weakening status is not exclusively related to the turbulence experienced in the global economy unleashed by the financial crisis and the role the United States had played in its emergence, or, on the other side, to a growing importance of China. The reasons, instead, seem much more profound.[9]

- The competitiveness of economies of the key countries of the West is on a slump. The balance increasingly shifts to the benefit of countries of the entire Asian zone. While the American economy – just as some economies of the Euro Area states – still reveals a high level of innovation and abilities of adaptation, still their advantage in these areas is visibly shrinking.[10] A true revolution in shale gas extraction and the achievements the United States have recently had in this field managed to improve this country' condition to a certain extent but this is no promise for the trend to persist in the future.
- The hitherto-existing consumer society ethos becomes undermined. It has been based upon 3 mainstays: intensive labour – higher rate of savings – permanent capital accumulation. It was partially thanks to this ethos that the foundations of highly developed capitalist states were built, featuring high level of welfare and social security.[11]

---

7 Ferguson N., "Czy kres cywilizacji Zachodu?" (A Decline of Western Civilisation?), *EUROPA*, December 2010.

8 Stiglitz J., (2009), "Capitalistic Fools", *Vanity Fair*, January, 2009.

9 Ferguson N., "Czy kres cywilizacji Zachodu?" (A Decline of Western Civilisation?).

10 Nowak A.Z., "Współczesny świat w erze turbulencji" (Contemporary World at the Time of Turbulence).

11 *ibid.*

- Work ethics ceases to be an absolute priority. One factor that is clearly detrimental to that traditional value is, among other things, an increasing conviction that there is less and less relationship between the sense of additional effort and relevant financial reward achieved. Indeed the degeneration witnessed in financial markets in this respect had and still has exerted tremendously negative effects upon social awareness in terms of ethics and morality. It becomes more and more common attitude to believe that the incomes earned on earnest work are totally incomparable to profits potentially made in stock exchange or through all sorts of speculative behaviours[12].
- We are witnessing the emergence, on a massive scale, of a phenomenon of cyber-terrorism, i.e. the use of achievements of information technologies to cause damage from political, ideological and, more and more often, also economic motives to states and to businesses and its infrastructure, especially that essential for the economy.
- At the same time, a threatening crisis of the authority of the state and the rule of law becomes evident in many countries of Western civilisation. Until now it was universally recognised that liberal democracy, the rule of law and civil society add up to the best possible measure against a temptation of political destabilisation. However, in the most recent financial crisis, extremely demoralising manifestations of helplessness or sometimes partial guilt of political authorities for the condition of the state and its crucial institutions – including those which went out of control – provoked massive social protests and riots questioning the authority of government and very foundations of legal order.[13]

New Patterns for Development – the End of the Washington Consensus?

An increasing group of economists as well as politicians believe that many of the problems that have emerged on the global scale should lead to search for new solutions and for a new economic deal, no longer relying solely on the USA, the European Union or Japan, but instead also considering the interests and power of new economic forces such as ASEAN, MERCOSUR, China, India, Brazil, Mexico, i.e. the so-called emerging economies. According to them, other, even

---

12 *ibid.*

13 Nowak A.Z.,"Współczesny świat w erze turbulencji" (Contemporary World at the Time of Turbulence).

more significant systemic transformations could alter the hitherto-existing development patterns in the global economy.

For several recent decades the theory of economy has been dominated by the so-called Washington Consensus. Rather than coming only from academic studies, it originated from real trends occurring in the process of globalisation. These megatrends in the global economy mainly include the following:[14]

Deregulation

Deregulation which means legal, organisational and regulatory actions leading to restriction of the influence and control the state and its institutions have upon economic life and the public sphere. In practice, deregulation leads to an increased role of market in commercial activity and hence also to maximisation of profit as its fundamental objective. Less and less controlled corporative style of management and decision-making implies that real authority in the area of crucial economic decisions is in the hands of presidents or boards of directors of companies, in many cases having supranational status. However, deregulation also brought some measurable positive results, in such respects as, among others:

- Internationalisation of production and distribution,
- Modern technologies transfer,
- IT revolution,
- The emergence of new markets.

Liberalisation

Liberalisation is strongly linked to the process of globalisation, to which a free movement of products, production factors, technologies, capital, and people is central, as well as a relocation and redefinition of institutions and companies to a supranational level. One consequence of market operation on the global scale is elimination of barriers in global economy, in particular in international trade, but also gradual abolition of restrictions in the transfer of capital and financial resources.

Liberalisation also has a significant influence upon the process of extension of economic freedom in many parts of the world and in practice leads to dissemination of the market economy model typical of states having considerable traditions of free market such as the United States or the United Kingdom.

---

14 *ibid.*

Privatisation

Privatisation is an economic process leading to the taking over of social or national property by private entities in order to make more effective use of production potential through creation of the stronger motivation supposed to result from the right of ownership.[15] One characteristic feature of the new global economy is the dominance of private property, largely stemming from the doctrine the modern foundations of which were laid down by Professor Milton Friedman. According to it, the principal factor that influences the condition of economy and its development over shorter or longer periods is the supply of money, and the government should restrict its influence upon the economy to supervision over this supply and to the establishment of constant and clear economic rules giving preference to private ownership[16]. The doctrine of ultra liberalism, of which M. Friedman was the most prominent exponent, restricting the role of state in the economy and diminishing the importance of public sector has been a significant element of systemic transformation in some countries with emerging economies (e.g. Chile).

Integration

Integration is about bringing any individuals, groups, institutions, regions or states together and creating common, uniform bodies out of them – in other words, joining or merging. In a narrower meaning this is an economic and political process the aim of which is to provide conditions for the optimum economic development of states and regions, for pursuit and securing of their various interests and for deepening of the awareness of the common system of values that keeps them together.[17]

The best example of integration in the latter sense is given by the history of the European Union. A milestone in the EU development was the establishment in 1987 of the Single (internal) Market, which gave a European response to the challenges brought by the process of economic globalisation. Another important stage of European integration was creation of the Euro Area in which the common currency Euro was introduced, supervised by the European Central Bank having its seat in the Frankfurt am Main. In other parts of the world we can cite the examples of ASEAN and MERCOSUR as regional blocs for the promotion of economic and political cooperation.

---

15 Source: Polish Language Dictionary.

16 Friedman M., *Capitalism and Freedom*. Chicago: University Of Chicago Press. November 15th, 2002.

17 Source: Foreign Words Vocabulary.

Under conditions of globalisation, however, the scope of the notion of integration is not just confined to states. It also relates to the actions of private institutions and companies as well as of governments, which coordinate – or even manipulate – key sectors of the global economy such as production and trade in some strategic raw materials, or energy.[18]

These four principal trends seen in the global economy, i.e.: deregulation, liberalisation, privatisation and integration, have become the crucial canon for economic policy of a number of states. It is in this area that the above-mentioned Washington Consensus was prevailing until recently. This term was coined by John Williamson – director of the Institute for International Economics in Washington. The four mega-trends were assumed, most of all, to favour the following:[19]

1. Maintenance of financial discipline so that budgetary deficit was relatively minor or at best fully balanced.
2. Implementation of tax reform so that it also becomes another impulse for economic growth.
3. Financial liberalisation (whose ultimate objective is for the market to fix interest rates).
4. Unifying of currencies' exchange rates, for commercial transactions at least, and their fixing at a level ensuring development of new economy sectors so that a sustainable competitiveness is ensured.
5. Liberalisation of global trade principles.
6. Abolition of barriers for foreign direct investments so that foreign businesses can compete with domestic ones at par terms.
7. Carrying out privatisation and – on a narrower scale – commercialisation.
8. Ensuring deregulation, which eliminates provisions preventing market entry and restricting competition due to reasons other than security.
9. Restriction of supervision over financial institutions and financial markets.
10. Protection of property rights with a legal system structured in a way that possession implies no excessive costs.

These fundamental guidelines for economic policy were undergoing certain modifications over time. However, their core essentially remained unchanged. They have become the principal development pattern for many countries. The turnaround moment that verified the arrangements of the "Washington Consensus"

---

18 Nowak A.Z., "Współczesny świat w erze turbulencji" (Contemporary World at the Time of Turbulence).

19 Nowak A.Z., "Współczesny świat w erze turbulencji" (Contemporary World at the Time of Turbulence).

came in the form of the financial crisis of the years 2007–2009 – unexpected both in terms of its scale and range. Its consequences have reached far beyond its initial period. Many of the theoretical assumptions of economic theories relying upon the belief in self-regulating repair mechanisms of free market, failed to work. Moreover, the system, deprived of regulating mechanisms, began to produce all sorts of degenerations. Among them, mistakes and distortions emerging in financial markets proved especially damaging both for the economic system and for ordinary people within it.

New financial instruments created in the American subprime real estate market turned out to be an enormous speculative bubble. It was these that initiated the explosion of the financial crisis in the United States. Deregulation in the banking system also caused, along with some positive effects, highly negative effects as well. In response to the trend of loanable funds (financial capital) searching for assets, banks began to expand into non-banking areas of activities, such as investment banking and assets management services. These new areas of the sector operation, oriented to prompt and high profit, contributed to generation of the so-called toxic assets which led some of the USA's great banks, insurance institutions and assets management companies to bankruptcy. The real estate market, a crucial one in the USA given the high levels of home ownership, was the one to suffer the most. The costs of the turbulence were mainly borne by American taxpayers.[20]

Quite a peculiar role in the global economic crisis was – and still is – played by three American credit rating agencies known as the Big Three. They are:

Standard&Poor's, Moody's, and Fitch Ratings.

Rating agencies are private institutions, which assess the reliability of various securities issuing business or public entities: companies, funds, banks, organisations and state governments, by analyzing the likelihood of their timely repayment of credits with interest. The analysis also covers an assessment of entities' credibility as borrowers and as issuers of long- and short-term securities.

The above-mentioned agencies were regarded as the guarantors of financial credibility – but in fact in the lead-up to the 2008 crisis they largely vouched for the soundness of an array of financial institutions, banks in particular, although these were in a critical situation at the time, often at the verge of bankruptcy. What should be seen as extremely shocking is the fact that none of the three faced any consequences of their actions, which were disastrously misleading in many cases.

20 Nowak A.Z., "Współczesny świat w erze turbulencji" (Contemporary World at the Time of Turbulence).

Today the problem of overcoming the problems revealed by the global financial crisis rests with individual governments. State budgets are mostly very tight from one country to another in many of them all applicable limits of expenditure excess over revenues (i.e. public sector budget deficits) were transgressed. All this in a situation where the contemporary state with its budget is also responsible for four fundamental spheres of public life, namely: education, health care and health safety, social security and security of the state and its citizens.[21] Under conditions of crisis, with public finance and many financial institutions at the very edge, the state and more specifically the governments faced with high budgetary deficits have to decide where to allocate their limited resources – in other words, they have to specify their priorities.

The government of the United States, where first manifestations of the global financial crisis were seen, had to make extremely difficult decisions. Through the American central bank, i.e. the Federal Reserve (Fed) the government applied a therapy of Quantitative Easing, i.e. increased supply of money, mainly directed at the banking sector.

Quantitative Easing (QE) is a policy applied by central banks consisting in massive buying of central government's or local government' bonds or mortgage-backed securities (MBS) from commercial banks. Unlike budgetary deficits, QE brings no change to net assets level in the private sector. Therefore, it makes a monetary policy rather than fiscal policy instrument. Stimulation achieved through increased quantity of money in circulation fosters consumption and demand, which should in turn translate into increased production, employment and wages.

The ultimate goal of Fed's operation was to stimulate the economy and to rebuild its reliability in financial markets. This therapy in the true spirit of John Maynard Keynes contributed to controlling of the financial crisis in the United States, but it also resulted in an increased public debt. That's why the Fed, under the new direction of Mrs. Janett Yellen, the first woman head in the history of American central bank, commenced an operation consisting in gradual withdrawal from the program of mass bond redemption.

Federal Reserve (Fed) is one the world's most influential central banks. Since the outbreak of the financial crisis in 2008 its role has increased enormously as it was involved in prevention of even more serious real breakdown of the US economy and hence of economies around the world and of global financial system.

---

21 Kaletsky A., *Capitalism 4.0. The Birth of a New Economy in the Aftermath of Crises*, Amazon 2010, p. 130.

The supply of the economy with cheap money achieved through monthly buy-ins of long-term bonds was intended to reduce the interest on long-term credits.

Globalisation - European Perspective

The financial crisis of the years 2007–2009 and aftermath had its source in the United States but very soon it became a global crisis. Actually, it was economies of European countries that suffered the most as they recorded serious declines of their gross domestic products. For many European Union member states overcoming the recession generated social as well as economic problem, the more so that consequences of the financial crisis infected from the United States also revealed weaknesses inherent in mechanisms of Euro Area operation.[22]

The establishment of the common currency (Euro) area was intended to accelerate economic growth in the less developed countries of the EU. These have mainly included countries of Southern Europe. To begin a mechanism of convergence was to be achieved by free markets. Less developed countries enjoyed some comparative advantages in the form of lower wages, larger labour resources and lower capital saturation. This translated into an advantageous pattern:

- Cheap unused resources and factors of production from the South;
- Abundance of capital in Northern countries of Euro Area;
- Low interest rates and readily available credit.

It was predicted that these factors should have stimulated the rate of economic growth of underdeveloped countries and would lead, over time, to equalisation of GDP levels throughout the Euro Area. Admittedly, wealthy Northern countries were also expected to benefit from more dynamic development in the South.

Unfortunately, these hopes failed to become reality. The investments made – and more broadly the streams of loanable funds (capital) flow – were quite often mismanaged by the invisible hand of the free market. Instead of the desired convergence, what happened (and is still occurring) is actually divergence. Economies of countries of the South became uncompetitive, both with respect to those of the North of the EU and to their other trade partners.[23]

Directions of advisable changes intended to correct the way the Monetary Union operates and preferred methods of overcoming the present crisis stem from diverging

22 Nowak A. Z, "Współczesny świat w erze turbulencji" (Contemporary World at the Time of Turbulence), p. 54.

23 Nowak A. Z, Ryć, K., "Europa potrzebuje liberalnego Keynesa" (Europe Needs A Liberal Keynes), *Rzeczpospolita*, 26 November 2013.

assessments of the reasons believed to have caused the crisis. We may distinguish two different interpretations of reasons behind the Monetary Union's systemic crisis, revealed under conditions of global economy crisis.

- The first reason indicates irresponsibility of some governments, which allowed for an excessive growth of public and/or private sector indebtedness. Consequences of that were fully exposed by the crisis. As a result, countries ruled by irresponsible politicians lost the trust of financial markets. It is therefore irresponsible policy on the part of many governments, their mistakes and omissions rather than markets that proved decisive and therefore should be held guilty of the situation we have faced.
- Another viewpoint emphasises serious gaps in the way the Euro system has been structured and its flawed implementation – defects not really revealed over the period of upswing in the business cycle and fully exposed only when the global crisis hit. This reason is also indicated as lending evidence to arguments raised by many sceptics doubting whether it was reasonable to implement the project of Euro Area establishment in the first place due to insufficient *real* convergence of the component economies of the Eurozone. This attitude is found in a number of American economists, but it was also expressed earlier on in academic circles in Europe.[24]

The process of Euro Area economies divergence has already become reality, but it is an even greater problem that this phenomenon may get even worse. How is it possible to counteract this process of divergence? The question is asked in awareness that it is crucial to counteract it, as further drifting or – according to the most pessimistic scenario – dissolution of the Euro Area would become truly dramatic, also for operation of the entire European Union. Are changes in regulatory system and the measures applied in European banking system sufficient to overcome the crisis of trust in financial markets? These questions remain open.

The need to restore stability to the financial sector in the Union, while not an easy task by any measure as this concerns budgetary condition of a number of states seems imperative. However, reforms made so far, with an evident prevalence of fiscal solutions, may expose Europe to long-lasting political and social conflicts. Contrary to what people believe, it isn't certain at all, whether these solutions will lead to raised efficiency and productivity and in effect to better competitiveness of many Euro Area member states. If they fail to, Europe's position would

24 Dornbusch R., *Keys to Prosperity: Free Markets Sound Money and a Bit of Luck*, Cambridge: MIT Press, 2000. p. 45.

deteriorate compared to such global economic powers as USA, India, China or, recently, Mexico.

At present the principal problem, it seems, is about the choice of a path to follow to restore growth trends in the European Union. An opinion, which is increasingly heard, is that a new vision is needed in the area of economic policy. The strategy of improvement of competitiveness and acceleration of economic and social growth should also include a combination and – in certain cases – also intensified continuance of actions in favour of support of various sectors in the EU member states. An active, but, despite all things, also well-defined role of state is not only not going to harm, but indeed will help in the process of overcoming a very complex, socially dramatic economic situation in many countries.[25]

The strong position of the European Community, so desirable nowadays, will enable it to run a more dynamic common trade policy. In June 2012 the EU signed, with six countries of Central America[26] an agreement on association including comprehensive regulations in the area of political, development-related and commercial cooperation. The agreement fitted quite well with current trends to foster trade relationships through establishment of free trade zones. While the potential effects of the agreement may actually turn out to be more significant for the economies of Central American countries than for the European Union, still it reflects certain intent to secure interests of the EU and its member states in this region.[27]

A project, which seems even more ambitious, is that of free trade agreement to be made between the United States and the European Community. As intended – and provided it finally becomes reality – this will be the world's largest free trade zone. Whereas the process of globalisation as well as the treaties concerning multilateral negotiation about world trade (World trade Organisation WTO treaties) lead to countries' opening to trade exchange and to foreign investments, still in the case of the United States and the European Union complex customs tariffs systems and overlapping legislation restrict the practical scale of commercial exchange. This has negative effects upon generation of economic growth and new jobs creation.

---

25 Nowak, A.Z., Shachmurove Y., (2012), "End of Eurozone?", in: *Understanding Global Economy – National and Regional Studies,* The Faculty of Management, Warsaw: University of Warsaw Press.

26 Guatemala, Honduras, Costa Rica, Nicaragua, Panama, Salvador.

27 Mazur G., "Układ Stowarzyszeniowy Unia Europejska- Ameryka Środkowa" (European Union – Central America Association Agreement), *Unia Europejska*, 5(222), 2013.

The EU is the world's biggest trader, accounting for 16,5 % of the world's imports and exports. Free trade among its members was one of the EU's founding principles. **EU trade policy is made exclusively at EU level.** The Commission negotiates agreements on behalf of the EU within WTO rules and works closely with national governments and the European Parliament to maintain the global system and enable it to adapt to worldwide changes. That's why the EU is committed to liberalising world trade as well.

Source: Europe EU site, Trade, 2014, based on: http://europa.eu/pol/comm/index_en.htm.

USA: quoting from data of the U.S. Department of Commerce, the total value of the United States' export and import in 2012 amounted to USD 3.82 trillion. The United States have been the world's third largest exporter following China and Germany. In 2013 the EU, as second largest trade partner after Canada, participated in 17% of the total American export, while in terms of import it also ranked second in 2013, following China and having 16% share in total U.S. import. **United States are the world's largest importer**.

Source: Trading Economics.com. 04.02.2014.

Data concerning trade exchange between 27 EU member states and the USA in the years 2009–2011 indicate that the EU has a surplus in trade which increased, over the period of these three years, from EUR 51.5 billion to EUR 76.3 bn.

Figure 1.1: Data concerning trade exchange between 27 EU member states and the USA in the years 2009–2011.

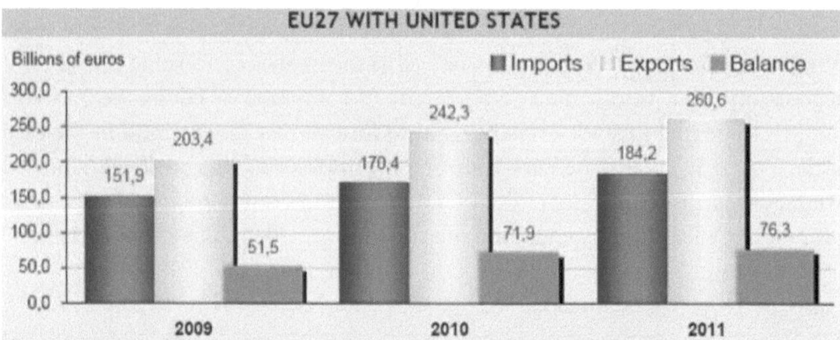

Source: http://trade.ec.europa.eu/doclib/docs/2006/september/tradoc_113465.pdf.

Respective levels of economic development, complementarity, political, social, and cultural proximity as well as similar potentials made the USA and EU natural partners in a more and more liberalised world trade environment. However, the way to the ultimate conclusion of the free trade agreement is not going to be easy, considering the diverging interests (especially of vested interests) that both parties have as well.

Conclusions

Fast-paced globalisation is a profound, multi-faceted and complex process. The explanatory challenges it poses include identification of crucial driving factors, trends and mechanisms behind it as well as consequences it brings. This study addressed some of the factors we reckon to be fundamental.

One phenomenon, which seems of particular importance, namely the impact and influence globalisation has upon financial markets, was discussed repeatedly, in a number of contexts. Financial markets are, as emphasised, among the significant sources of excessive financialisation of the world economy, thus causing negative consequences, too. Despite all that, contemporary globalism, or capitalism for that matter, is still and rather fortunately not a classic casino. However, we have grown more and more aware now that whilst Adam Smith may have been right in arguing that free market is the best form of economy and its extremely important regulator, it is also very true that not all decisions made in the global market are necessarily leading to expected and desirable effects. It is mainly businesses that have to reckon with this, as they cannot put their money on ready-made models or seemingly proven instruments and ways of overcoming crisis situations. Anyway, generation of new and original knowledge, its use and dissemination is probably the most effective way for innovative development of both enterprises and societies. It is probably the right way for Poland as well – a country that has certainly been beneficiary of the globalisation processes to a higher extent than it has been an outsider left behind. Under conditions of globalisation there is no room for further doubts that states are going to be able to face many challenges purely on their own. Conceived as "federal union," the EU could give an adequate answer to such challenges in the future. Rather than being perceived as an exterminator of national states, the European Union could prove capable of providing them with proper conditions for survival within the globalised world. For this to happen, however, first the EU may need to be politically reformed enough to stand up to this complex task.

Bibliography

De Grauwe, P. (2009), *Economics of Monetary Union*, Oxford: Oxford University Press.

Dornbusch R. (2000), *Keys to Prosperity: Free Markets Sound Money and a Bit of Luck*, Cambridge: MIT Press.

Edvinsson L. (2012), "Universal Networking, Intellectual Capital", in: *European Integration Process in the Regional and Global Settings*, Latoszek E., Kotowska I., Nowak A. Z., Stępniak A. (eds.), Warsaw: University of Warsaw School of Management Press.

Ferguson N. (2010), "Czy kres cywilizacji Zachodu?" (A Decline of Western Civilisation?), *EUROPA*.

Kaletsky A. (2010), *Capitalism 4.0. The Birth of a New Economy in the Aftermath of Crises*, Amazon.

Kenen P.B., (1995), *Economic and monetary union in Europe: Moving beyond Maastricht*, Cambridge: Cambridge University Press.

Kozioł W. (2004), "Wpływ globalizacji rynków finansowych na przebieg kryzysów finansowych" (Financial Markets Globalisation Impact Upon the Process of Financial Crises), in: *Wyzwania globalizacji. Odpowiedzi przedsiębiorstw* (*Globalisation Challenges. Entrepreneurs Replies*), Koładkiewicz I., Kozioł W. (eds.), Warsaw: University of Warsaw School of Management Press.

Krugman P. (2008), *The Return of Depression Economics and the Crisis of 2008*, USA: W.W. Norton & Company Inc.

Krugman P. (2011), "Can Europe Be Saved?", USA, *New York Times Magazine*.

Legrain Ph. (2010), *Aftershock: Reshaping the World Economy after Crisis*, London: Little Brown.

Lutkowski K., "Co się stało w strefie euro?" (What Happened in the Euro Area?), *Rzeczpospolita*, 15 June 2012.

Mazur G. (2013), "Układ stowarzyszeniowy Unia Europejska-Ameryka Środkowa" (European Union – Central America Association Agreement), European Union, 5(222).

Morawski W. (2004), "Mapy drogowe globalizacji: Propozycje analityczno-teoretyczne" (Globalisation Road Maps), in: *Wyzwania globalizacji. Odpowiedzi przedsiębiorstw* (*Globalisation Challenges. Entrepreneurs' Replies*), Koładkiewicz I., Kozioł W. (eds.), Warsaw: University of Warsaw School of Management Press.

Nowak A.Z., Ryć K. (2014), "Real Convergence as the Way to Heal the Euro Area?", *Rzeczpospolita*, 2014.

Nowak A.Z., Shachmurove Y. (2012), "End of Euro Area?", in: *Understanding Global Economy – National and Regional Studies*, Warsaw: University of Warsaw School of Management Press.

Nowak, A.Z. (2007), *European Economic Integration: Chances and Challenges*. Warsaw: University of Warsaw School of Management Press.

Prahalad C. K., Krishnan M. S. (2010), *Nowa era innowacji* (*The New Age of Innovation: Driving Co-Created Value Through Global Networks*), Warsaw: PWN.

Ravenhill J. (2005), *Global Political Economy*, Oxford: Oxford University Press.

Soros G. (05.2008), "*Markets: The New Paradigm for Financial Markets: The Credit Crisis of 2008 and What It Means*", USA: Public Affairs.

Stiglitz J. E. (2009), "Capitalistic Fools", *Vanity Fair*.

Stiglitz J. E. (2010), *Can the Euro be Saved?*, Project Syndicate. http://www.project-syndicate.org/commentary/stiglitz125/English.

Stojano A. (2009), *Research, Quality, Competitiveness. European Union Technology Policy for the Knowledge-Based Society*, Springer Science+Business Media, 2nd edition.

Taplin R., Nowak A.Z. (eds.) (2010), *Intellectual Property, Innovation and Management in Emerging Economies*, London: Routledge.

Tidd J., Bessant J. (2011), *Zarządzanie innowacjami* (*Managing the Innovations*), Warsaw: Wolters Kluwer Publishing.

Part II

Patrick O'Sullivan

The Role of Failures of Morality in the Financial Crisis in Europe: Diagnosis and Implications

Introduction

That among the roots of the lingering financial crisis and its debt hangover there have been an array of moral failings on the part of a range of actors is by now well recognised and the chapter will begin by recalling and summarising some of these as well as noting that there has also been an epistemological failure at work which may or may not count as immoral: certain key actors simply did not understand what was happening systemically. We then look at the Eurozone debt crisis in particular and we shall discover a rich undercurrent of moral attitudes and issues reminiscent of a morality play in the way the sovereign debt crisis has been confronted in the Eurozone. Once the moral diagnosis is complete the chapter moves to look at what might be done to improve moral attitude and character in the financial sector noting the practical difficulty of such transformation; it will be suggested that while some of the regulations adopted by the European Union and the much maligned European Parliament have helped to address some of the Eurozone's failings in dealing with these problems in the EU and throughout the world there is a key role for education of all actors concerned; for a greater education in technical macroeconomics and finance (reflecting the cognitive failures), in Business Ethics and in a new discipline which I have called *Political Ethics.*

Moral Failings Underpinning the 2008 Financial Crisis

The story of how first the United States and subsequently Europe and the world suffered a catastrophic financial crisis in 2008 is now a familiar one and despite the remarkable lack of immediate understanding of what was happening in the financial *system as a whole* in the early 2000s, today we have a fairly detailed retrospective understanding of how the disaster happened. There is little doubt that among the contributing factors was an array of what we might call more or less immoral behaviour on the part of various key actors in the system. One hesitates to say *immoral* since it is a strong and evaluative word which presupposes some sort of moral code or code of virtue and as we all too obviously realise in today's world not everybody lies by the same moral code or code of virtue. Nonetheless, there are certain fundamental moral values, which are universal to all human beings because of their manifestly rational foundation, and which can be found in slightly different guises in all moral codes. Obvious examples are the moral condemnation of murder, of lying, of extortion; and the idea that law should be underpinned by natural justice. There may be differences of view about what is murder and what is justice, but what is clear is the fact that all human beings in some form or other subscribe to such values.

With these provisos in mind we may now identify some of the key elements of immorality, which have been held to have underpinned the financial crisis. Difficult to pin down exactly but undoubtedly identifiable as a key driving force behind the crisis was an insatiable materialist greed on the part of multitudes of actors. By greed here we mean not the desire for material prosperity which is natural (since we need to survive) and so morally neutral if not good; by greed we mean an excessive obsessive desire for the accumulation of ever more material wealth oblivious of the position or plight of other human beings around us in a manner that is entirely self-serving.[1] Such greed was and perhaps still is rampant and could be seen from the excessive outlandish salaries demanded by top financial executives before and even after the crisis right down to the behaviour of lowly junior market traders or even to mortgage sales representatives. This brings us to a second aspect not entirely confined to the financial sphere but very characteristic of the path that private sector capitalism took in the early 2000s: the huge gap which began to open up between the lowest paid workers in companies and their top or chief executives. There has been a sharp growth in inequality of remuneration within companies hugely exacerbated by a system of bonuses and golden handshakes. This to many seems patently unjust and unfair and it has been widely criticised both by politicians and in the academic literature.[2]

Another widely perceived area of immorality is in respect of the morality of the construction and selling of financial products of all kinds. On the one hand mortgage backed securities and other derivatives were being created from mixes of good and toxic assets (for example putting into a mortgage backed security some quality

---

1 Greed was of course recognised by the ancients as one of the 7 deadly sins. So Gordon Gekko in the movie Wall Street 1 was actually wrong: greed is not good.

2 See for example, Steiner P. (2011) *Les rémunérations obscènes: le scandale des hauts revenus en France*, Paris: La Découverte. See also in English the work of the same author in Fourcade M, Steiner P., Streeck W. and Woll C. (2013), "Moral Categories in the Financial Crisis", Max Po discussion paper 13/1, Paris: Max Planck Sciences Po Centre on Coping with Financial Instability. Steiner's piece is Chapter 2 at pp. 5–9.

loans and some loans very unlikely to perform, e.g. American subprime mortgages) and these were being sold on around the world to unsuspecting investors in some cases with the take it or leave it proviso[3] (in other words, buy it now as is or else forget it!) The morality of constructing such rubbish and then selling it on to unsuspecting buyers seems to many to be dubious to say the least. This is, in fact, a notorious grey area in the morality of marketing and selling. But, will come the reply then, what about the *caveat emptor* principle: let the buyer beware. Certainly the buyers of the various derivatives had a moral duty to enquire into the nature of what they were buying, in particular where they are agents acting on behalf of others (as with many institutional investors); and it can be argued as we will note below that many players did not make much serious effort to *inform* themselves in depth about what they were buying. It is a sad but inescapable fact that securitisation while no doubt having brought much greater flexibility to financial markets has also meant that banks and any other originators of high risk loans can get those loans and the risks they represent off their own books by securitisation: that is to say packing them up into derivatives and selling them on to the highest bidder (usually with a nice high credit rating from a rating agency: see below). How moral we may ask are such actions? Are they not much different from selling on an ostensibly fine but actually defective second hand car, which has crash stress damage to the chassis? And if the originators feel that they can sell on the high-risk loans (after earning fat initial commissions on the set-up, of course) will they even care about how reckless may be their lending (or how ultimately damaging for the borrower in the case of subprime mortgages)?

A major reason why so many buyers eagerly bought up derivative rubbish was because the three major rating agencies were eagerly giving top class ratings to the various mortgage backed securities. Since the rating agencies claim and are supposed to issue advice on the riskiness of all sorts of financial assets to have given the highest and second highest ranking on their silly letter scales to a huge range of mortgage backed securities and other derivative junk was at best the result of sheer and systematic incompetence if not (given their advisory role) a matter of criminal negligence.

Mention of the rating agencies ignominious role in the 2008 débacle leads us to another fundamental area of moral concern regarding the genesis of the crisis: *moral hazard*. Moral hazard is a notoriously difficult notion to define precisely and many moral hazards that arise on principal-agent relationships are not per se immoral

3 Such behaviour is worthy of the best car sales sharks or spivvy salesmen for property condominiums that are not yet built and may never be built. But it happened also in the financial sector.

but rather to do with misalignment of incentives. But certain types of moral hazard certainly do raise issues of morality, hence the term. In a previous work with Alojzy Z. Nowak we have sought to arrive at a definition of *immoral* moral hazards that at least is relevant to the financial sector. "Moral hazard becomes immoral when the incentive system that surrounds some set of transactions involves an inducement to one or more of the parties to act in an immoral manner."[4] When we apply this concept to the pre-2008 financial sector it is particularly fruitful. First of all the rating agencies faced an enormous moral hazard in that their fees for rating of securities were and still are paid by the issuer of the security to be rated[5]. In particular in an ambiance of oligopolistic rivalry among the 3 big rating agencies (which are private US-based firms) there was a temptation to overrate the securities, which the banks and other originators were constructing for onward sale. This was very akin to the grade inflation phenomenon, which has been experienced in American and other private sector universities over the past 50 years. The inducement to *immoral* behaviour was quite simply the incentive for the rating agencies to lie about the true quality of the toxic assets.

A second major area of moral hazard on which there has been extensive comment is in the role of central banks and financial regulators in the crisis. On the one hand we have an explicitly capitalist free market system as the dominant economic ideology at least over the vast majority of the developed Western economies and certainly including Canada, US, and EU, i.e. the states where the crisis originated and where its biggest impact was felt; and under this ideology firms are supposed to come and go as they become more or less profitable respectively: the law of the market reigns and that is supposed to produce an optimal allocation of resources[6]. Moreover in all of these states but especially in US and Britain there had been a systematic deregulation of the financial sector since the mid-1980s. This rolling back of the role of the state was supposedly to enhance the role of market forces in the sector and thereby to promote efficiency in the sector[7]. But side by side with this deregulation of the financial sector governments in particular through their

4 O'Sullivan P., Smith M., and Esposito M. (2012), *Business Ethics: a Critical Approach Integrating Ethics across The Business World*, London: Routledge. See ch. 11, p. 149.

5 Surprisingly up to the mid-1970s the rating agency fees were paid by the investors who needed advice, not by the issuers of the security. Such a system was devoid of moral hazard and had much to recommend it.

6 Of course, under a very restrictive set of conditions: perfect competition in all markets with well-informed economic agents and no externalities.

7 This was of course a central plank of the Reagan-Thatcher agenda for the whole economy when they came to power in the early 1980s in the US and UK respectively.

central banks were still expected to act as final guarantors of stability of the financial system by acting as lenders of last resort to the system. In short the central banks and/or governments stood ready to "bail out" the banking and financial system in the event of any serious systemic risk. The reason for retaining this role is simply that failures of financial institutions, especially big ones, tend to cause a huge shock to confidence in all financial institutions which in a fractional reserve system can quickly lead to a complete collapse of the whole system of credit and so of finance as people withdraw their cash wholesale from suspect institutions. In today's world if the banking and credit system fails the economy simply grinds to a halt.

But now we are in the presence of the mother of all moral hazards. On the one had the banks and other financial institutions are operating with minimal regulation in a capitalist free market system where it is widely presumed that the sole or at least overriding goal of firms is to maximise profits. The highest profits are potentially to be made in the most risky of assets/investments.

Bankers have every reason therefore to make very risky loans/fund high-risk investments; and, to be sure, if the central bank is there to act as lender of last resort the banker does not need to worry too much about scenarios where the loans/investments turn sour. This comfort blanket is all the stronger for the bigger institutions deemed to be "too big to be allowed to fail." So it was that a wide array of financial institutions became extremely reckless to the point of negligence in their lending precisely because of the lender of last resort guarantee. They then compounded this negligence by parcelling up the toxic loans and investments usually but not always with some better quality stuff into derivatives (mortgage backed securities) which they would then sell off to investors at large in what we have just seen was an arguably dishonest type of selling aided and abetted by the negligent rating agencies.

If the nature of the moral hazard is easy enough to see what is not necessarily so obvious is what to do about it; but of this more later when we come to deal with remedies for the immoralities we have detected in the sector. One key point to note at this stage however is that in the case of a moral hazard the moral culpability is *shared*. On the one hand there will be the immoral actions carried out by those who are tempted into such by the system of incentives. But we must also acknowledge the moral responsibilities of those who set up those incentive systems in the first place: they also bear a share of the moral blame. So in this case the immorality was not just on the side of those greedy evil bankers and financiers: there is also a portion of the

---

Deregulation in the City of London dates from the so-called "big bang" of 1985, a major offensive of deregulation of Britain's financial sector.

moral blame for the 2008 debacle and what followed it to be shared by the regulators given the nature and weaknesses of the regulatory system they had set up.

Another major concern about the immoralities of the 2008 financial crisis and once again directed at governments rather than financial actors regards the huge sums of government money involved in the bailouts that were necessary to restore confidence in the system as a whole and in particular banks who faced insolvency because of write-downs in the values of their asset portfolios. These have been detailed in many places[8] and suffice it to say that in terms of actual direct capital injections sums representing between 2% and 5% of GDP were found in a range of advanced countries while the hypothetical guarantees offered by governments represented far more than this. This quite bluntly involves a redistribution of wealth from the community at large to the financial sector. This has usually been defended as something over which governments have little choice given the importance of the financial system to the functioning of the general economy but it can be perceived as inequitable whatever about the efficiency arguments that can be used to defend it. The financial sector taken as a whole as those working within it (especially in senior positions) could hardly be seen to be poor or devoid of resources; and so in effect we have witnessed a hugely regressive redistribution of wealth which many would see as contrary to natural justice or equity.

In a recent reflection on the moral and other factors involved in the crisis Arnold Kling[9] has argued that in addition to some of the undeniable moral failings that underpinned there were also some significant epistemological failures: that is to say a simple incomprehension or ignorance on the part of major actors regarding what was infolding before their eyes in the financial system. He shows how numbers of key actors whether out of simple ignorance, bona fide optimism in market systems, unwillingness to question classical market fundamentalist beliefs or inability to think beyond their own limited sphere of activity to consider systemic risks and issues simply did not understand that mounting systemic fragility was rapidly being built up especially between 2001 and 2008. Some economists were all too aware of the growing risks in the system but nobody wanted to listen. However while Kling documents with a range of revealing quotations from various actors in the crisis how real and pervasive the incomprehension and thus cognitive failure was one has to ask the question also: was there not a moral failure also present in all of this? Ignorance may be bliss but when in positions of high responsibility where

8 See for example, O'Sullivan P., Smith M., Esposito M., (2012), ch 11, pp. 156–160.

9 Kling A., (2013) "The Financial Crisis: Moral Failure or Cognitive Failure?", in: Harvard Journal of law and Public Policy Vol. 33, pp. 507–518.

one's actions or inactions can have a profound effect on myriad human lives the ignorance can also amount to moral negligence. Many of those actors *should* have known better and *should* have taken the trouble better to inform themselves and to understand rather better the system in which they were playing such a key (and as it happens dangerously destructive) role. This consideration of morally irresponsible negligence applied above all to the rating agencies, in whom so many actors were placing their trust in seeking some indication of the riskiness of he ever more complex financial derivatives which they were trading.

Sovereign Debt Crisis in the Eurozone: Some Specific Moral Failings

Up to this point we have catalogued major moral failings that have underpinned the initial 2008 financial crisis. But as we know that crisis triggered a subsequent more specific crisis of sovereign debt management in a whole range of Eurozone countries which if abated is not yet entirely past. We now examine the extent to which there are some new or more specific moral failings underpinning that very European post crisis; or as we might with poetic licence say, the European hangover!

It is by now well understood that what the Eurozone has been facing over the period 2009–2013 is a debt or in particular a sovereign debt crisis. As a currency the Euro has not had a crisis in the sense that it has remained remarkably stable against other major currencies and has if anything been appreciating slightly against other major currencies for the past two years. This can readily be seen from a graph of the US Dollar $/Euro € spot exchange rate over the whole period from 2010 up to the present. (See Figure 3.1)

Figure 3.1: US$ dollars per €euro spot exchange rate from 2010 to 2014.

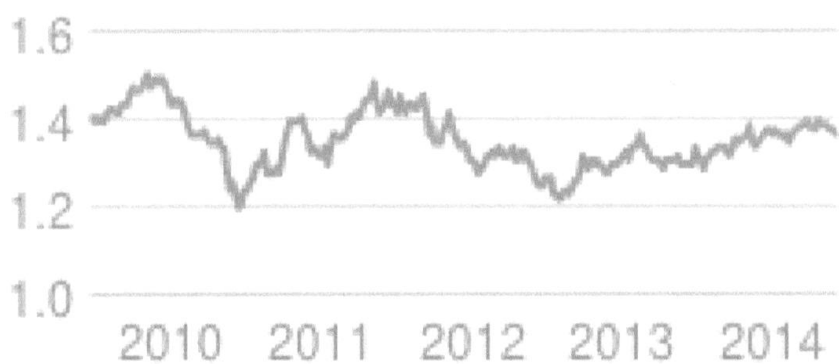

Source: Financial Times, London.

What the Eurozone has endured however is a debt crisis in both the private and especially public sectors. The debt crisis in the private sector (here we are referring to household and NGO debt, not to private sector business debt) is confined to about half of Eurozone states and as in the US this private debt crisis was in many cases intimately linked to a real estate bubble. In Ireland, United Kingdom, Spain, Portugal and Cyprus this was the case but there are other Eurozone states where the ratio of private sector debt to GDP is extremely high (in excess of 175%) but where there has not been a real estate bubble and burst in any significant sense: Denmark Sweden Netherlands and Luxembourg. In these latter states one can hardly speak of a private sector debt crisis as such since there has been no big asset price burst and loss of confidence although such high levels of private sector debt must act as a long term drag on consumption in the economies in question as private consumers seek gradually to pay down the debt.

Rather more high profile has been the problem of huge *public* sector indebtedness in a number of Eurozone countries, notably in Greece, Spain and Portugal and to a lesser extent Italy. Ireland also faced a public debt crisis but has now left that behind it after a period of wrenching austerity at least in public sector spending between 2009 and 2013. The precise extent of the public sector deficits and resultant borrowings and of the resulting accumulated public sector debt have been documented in other chapters of this work. Moreover Mark Blyth in his incisive work on the dangers of austerity as an idea has explained how in effect the public sector debt crisis grew in many cases out of the huge public sector spending to bail out banks in the aftermath of the 2008 financial crisis in the hardest hit European states (notably Ireland)[10]. To put this sovereign debt crisis into perspective we need to bear in mind firstly that when governments borrow to cover shortfalls between their spending and the receipts of taxation they may borrow from the private sector at large which however "crowds out" private sector investment by sucking loanable funds (savings) into government spending instead. Given that this is seen as undesirable if it occurs on a significant scale (and public sector borrowing could easily suck in between 10% and 40%[11] of all savings available even in economies where public sector borrowing is modest) it follows

10 See Blyth M., (2013) *Austerity: the History of a Dangerous Idea*, Oxford: Oxford University Press.

11 If the average propensity to save is 30% of GDP for example (a not untypical figure) and the public sector deficit is 3% of GDP then the government borrowing if all from the private sector would suck in already 10% of total available savings. If the public sector deficit is 6% of GDP, then the government borrowing would absorb 20% of total savings. 8% public sector deficit if the savings rate is 20% of GDP would mean that

that governments have tended to do the bulk of their borrowing from their central bank. This act of borrowing from the central bank *ipso facto* expands money supply of the economy.[12] It is worth recalling these elements of basic macroeconomic analysis to understand the Eurozone's current debt crisis and the "morality play" which has surrounded it.

The point is that for the Eurozone countries there is no national central bank to go to for borrowing: there is only the European Central Bank (ECB). Hence all of the Eurozone governments are in theory and in practice now borrowing from one and the same ECB; or as we might say feeding from the same trough! Imagine a family of 18 pigs each of whom had in the past individual troughs and many of whom have been used to feeding generously on food in their own individual troughs (central banks) that represented between 6% and 12% of their GDP. The pigs now find themselves at one and the same trough (ECB) with all of the other Eurozone pig family and where the food provisions in the trough are restricted to just 3% of GDP for the family of pigs as a whole. *Just imagine the jostling, grunting and squealing at the trough*!

This little parable is no doubt hilarious but it also gets right to the core of the Eurozone debt crisis problem and to the penumbra of moral problems surrounding it. The fact that such a range of countries, which are culturally quite diverse, should now all be reliant on one and the same central bank to meet their public sector borrowing needs was bound to lead to frictions. This is all the more true when we bear in mind that one of the key cultural differences lies in moral attitudes to borrowing and to debt as between these countries. These differences have become the basis of what Wolfgang Streeck has rightly likened to a kind of morality play narrative within which the duty to repay and the imperative of austerity to limit borrowing on the part of the Eurozone's big debt states is framed with surprisingly compelling moral force[13]. It is no accident that in German the word for debt is *Schuld* and the word for guilty is *schuldig*. So to a German way of thinking it is axiomatic that to be in debt is somehow to be (morally) guilty: I say *morally* because obviously one is not legally guilty if one has a debt: there is

---

the government was absorbing 40% of all savings. Borrowing from abroad may be an option but it carries its own political risks.

12 It is true that the central bank could neutralise this money supply expansion by open market operations to contract money supply…which means the central bank would sell back government securities to the private sector thereby generating the crowding out effect once again.

13 See Streeck W. (2013), in Fourcade M., Steiner P., Streeck W., and Woll C. (2013), ch. 4.

simply a legal liability to repay[14]. Similar even if not so explicit ideas can be found in certain other Northern European cultures and in certain more puritanical corners of American culture as well. Hence the debtors are somehow being implicitly cast as immoral: it is their duty to repay the generous creditors who lent to them at such advantageous rates. There is, it is being subtly suggested, a moral failing at the heart of the sovereign debt problems of the southern European states: it is the immorality of the feckless debtor who has borrowed recklessly and now cannot repay his generous creditor.

As Streeck so nicely points out, nowhere in this narrative so widely present in the media and in the statements of politicians of all stripes about the debt crisis does anybody ever question the morality of the "saintly" creditors. Were they perhaps negligently reckless in according the loans so carelessly in the first place? Is it morally acceptable to extort the last cent of every debt from unfortunate even if reckless borrowers? Moreover in the morality play of which the media and the Troika[15] are so fond it is the citizens of the debtor countries and *not* the politicians who oversaw the massive borrowings (and even deliberate distortion of public accounts) who are held liable to bear the burden of repayment. As Streeck comments in a cruel twist of an age-old democratic principle: for the Troika, *No taxation without representation* has become: *With representation (in democracies) full liability for citizens.*

Streeck's work and the perspective it brings to the question of morality in the Eurozone debt crisis are very important for a number of reasons. First of all by showing how underpinning the narrative of the Troika with its incantations about the need for "reform" there has been a more or less explicit morality play about debt and debtors playing out in the background he has shown us how central moral concerns and moral issues are in the whole phenomenon of the public sector debt crisis in the Eurozone. But with astute reflection Streeck has also shown us that the moral issues are by no means as black and white as the dominant morality play tends to suggest. Just as much as creditors may insist that it is right and proper that debtors should repay their debts we may ask about the moral responsibilities of the creditors who accorded the loans so recklessly in the first place? We have already seen above how securitisation in general has generated some serious moral issues insofar as it meant that the originators of high risk loans could afford to be as reckless as they pleased, since they would get

14 Legal guilt would arise only if payment of the debt becomes (seriously) overdue.

15 The Troika refers to that formidable gang of three: the IMF, ECB and European Commission who come to investigate the public accounts of debtor countries and then have the impertinence to suggest politico-economic "reforms": or else…

the loans off their books through securitisation; and that this offloading generates moral issues regarding possible deception in selling and marketing. In the context of the public sector debts and borrowings of the Eurozone these reflections on the duties of the creditors or buyers of securities to inform themselves (and not to rely blindly on rating agencies) paint a rather different picture of the moral responsibilities than those of the Troika morality play. Large quantities of Greek government bonds had been bought up by banks and other financial institutions in Northern European states, notably in Germany and France! How reckless had those banks and institutions been? Did they not understand the macroeconomics that the Troika so regularly preaches?

Streeck has then finally thrown up the deeply disturbing moral stance involved in laying the ultimate burden of adjustment to resolve the public sector debt crisis entirely on the people at large in the debtor countries through wrenching austerity policies. Quite apart from the fact that there can be a doubt to say the least as to whether austerity is the right macroeconomic policy in these circumstances in Europe[16] (and if it is not the right policy than people in Greece, Portugal, Italy, Spain are being made to endure severe hardships for nothing as have the Irish in the period 2009–2013), with the current austerity policies that have been imposed by the Troika in a number of states, in effect people and taxpayers at large are being made to pay a heavy price for a problem which they did not make. The reckless borrowing sprees and in some cases (Greece) deliberate distortion of the public accounts (aided, of course, by Goldman Sachs advice on securitisation!) was the work of politicians, senior public bureaucrats and their venal financial advisors. Is it then fair that the burden of the adjustments now being imposed should be borne by the people at large in Greece? Of course, it is true in some sense that a people get the government they deserve in a representative democracy. But should not he politicians and their advisors that led them into the abyss not at the very least be entirely banned from public office on grounds of incompetence if not in prison?[17] Sadly in some cases the self-same politicians have come back

16 See for example, Blyth M (2013), passim. See also the manifold pronouncements of wide ranges of economists including for example Paul Krugman and Joseph Stiglitz against austerity policies. See for example Krugman (2013), "How the Case for Austerity has Crumbled", in: *New York Review of Books*, 6 June 2013. Available at http://www.nybooks.com/articles/archives/2013/jun/06/how-case-austerity-has-crumbled/.

17 Representative democracy is supposedly a system that generates accountability of politicians, and, in principle perhaps, it does: the rogues can be voted out of office by a well-informed populace. But herein lies the catch. Representative democracy has to an increasing extent become a media show, not a real debate on politicians' records

to power. Should we therefore be surprised if so much of the European electorate has become so cynical of the whole political process? *A plague on all their houses* is in effect a common refrain especially among the young.

What Can We do About Moral Failings in the Crisis: Moral Improvements?

If the best critique should always be constructive and not just destructive it is incumbent on us now to ask: how can we overcome the identified moral failings for the future? However making recommendations for improvement in morality is a rather different matter from making recommendations as to economic policies or regulations since morality is not just another lever of socio-economic policy that can be manipulated at will as we might manipulate taxes or regulations on food safety standards. At the risk of stressing the obvious morality is a matter of a person's character and values and it is typically acquired through a long process first of socialisation at home and in school and then through experimentation and experience as the person matures. Of course, people can be persuaded to change their moral views (and if not we would never have been able to overcome mass slavery and systematic racial discrimination for example); but to change moral views is a long drawn out process that relies quite heavily on the educational process and on frank and open debate. That is why as a consensus begins to form legal regulation can be brought into play alongside persuasion to give people a legal incentive to behave in a more morally responsible manner. As we shall see it has been widely suggested that better regulation is a key element in the response to many of the identified moral failings in contemporary finance but we need to be careful not to overstate what it can achieve. Regulation which is not accompanied by at least a gradual change of moral conviction leads only to cynical evasion of the relevant regulations, a phenomenon endemic in the cat and mouse game between financiers and regulators that has all too often been observed in practice.

---

and the winning or losing of elections depends heavily on media coverage and indeed media preferences especially where a media outlet takes a partisan line. This is true even of the supposedly most robust democracies: witness the inordinate influence of the Murdoch owned press and media channels in the UK and the supine craven behaviour of UK politicians towards his media especially in the run-up to elections. Where elections become so dominated by partisan media and hence by the tycoons who invariably lie behind them how can the populace hope to be well informed and thus to hold the politicians accountable?

Recklessness and greed

One of the most fundamental moral failings underpinning the behaviour of wide ranges of actors in the financial crisis was as we saw an excess of greed. While it would certainly be ideal to try to address this by seeking to raise he moral standards and awareness of all actors in the financial sector from the highest executives down to the lowly traders and sellers of financial products a healthy (as opposed to a cynical) realism suggests that it will prove very difficult ever to eradicate greed entirely from human behaviour since we are not perfect saints and probably never will be. Moreover, Bernard Mandeville's *Fable of the Bees*[18] comes to mind. That is not to say however that it is futile to hope for an improvement of moral standards in finance through offering or even requiring a significant level of education in moral philosophy and in particular in business and finance schools for example. Let us be quite blunt about this: if there were more upstanding people of high moral integrity at the heart of the financial sector we would have far less self-serving greedy excesses and sharp practices, the latter often worthy of the most ruthless back street sharks and money lenders.

But if human beings are not saints we cannot just rely on moral education to remedy the failings: government regulation also has a key role to play in cleaning up the sector. In fact a wide array of new regulations have been proposed to regulate for example proper disclosure when selling financial products, rules for the granting of mortgages, tighter regulation of executive bonuses. The European Union is, of course, in the process of implementing its banking union regulations as described elsewhere in this volume. Moreover the European Parliament has recently passed regulations to cap banker's bonuses at levels deemed to be fair and equitable[19]. Thus regulation has a key role to play in dealing with greed and recklessness both in the EU (which has taken somewhat of a lead in this) and in the world as a whole.

Deception in selling of financial products

A second area of moral failing we unearthed was in respect of outright deception in the selling of financial products. This deception can occur at two levels: firstly at the lowly level of selling complex financial products such as subprime mortgages

18 Mandeville B. (1732), "The Fable of the Bees or Private Vices Public Benefits", Oxford: Clarendon Press. Available online at http://oll.libertyfund.org/.

19 A bonus cap was passed as part of the wider Capital Requirements Directive 4 of the EU by the European Parliament in April 2013. It had already been approved by the Council of Ministers so now has the force of a full blown EU Directive.

to poorer people who may have little or no understanding of finance. Of course, the slick sales rep can come back and say "well, *caveat emptor*, let the buyer beware" and indeed that is not beside the point. But let Mr. or Ms. Slick Sales Rep ask themselves a simple moral question; were they hoping that the unfortunate poor person would be fooled into buying something that is not good for them? Remember that the moral failure of lying is the *intent to deceive*. This type of basic moral failing is again difficult to eradicate by education alone especially given the educational attainment of many working at the low end of financial product sales. Hence strict regulation for example with cooling off clauses in loan and insurance contracts are an obvious way to deal with such problems but given the persistence of these types of abuse they are not perhaps all that effective. What is needed alongside the cooling off types of provision are outright regulations of the permissible features of financial products and/or of access to them. For example many countries in the Eurozone now actually regulate quite strictly access to mortgages with rules regarding maximum percentage of capital value of the asset that can be borrowed and/or maximum ratios as between the regular income of the mortgagee and the mortgage repayment.

Much higher up the scale of deceptive selling of financial products we encounter the issues surrounding the sales of complex derivatives to supposedly sophisticated traders and investors. Here again the sellers must ask themselves if there is intent to deceive[20] but now *caveat emptor* has a lot more relevance as a moral injunction to the buyers of the derivatives and other complex securities. We have noted following Kling that there have been some major cognitive failures underpinning the crisis and so it would follow that proper education of those involved in finance could make a significant contribution to avoiding these sorts of abusive sales. Note that here we are not talking of education in moral philosophy (although that is also of curse desirable in this connection) but rather of a real education in risk modelling, risk assessment, economics and political economy as opposed to the rote learning of formulaic approaches in a totally or largely uncritical manner such as has become common in all too many finance courses in business schools. With such a better and more critically based theoretical education it might be hoped that finance professionals would be a little less gullible and a bit more careful and aware when they buy derivative assets of all sorts.

At this higher level of dealing in financial derivatives among effectively finance "professionals" of various sorts it is not so clear if regulation can do much to deal

20 And indeed there was! As mentioned earlier many mortgage backed securities and other derivative junk were being sold off in instant sales on a take it or leave it basis.

with the possible abuses precisely because of the cat and mouse game between finance professionals and their regulators that has already been mentioned: regulate and the financial markets will react simply by inventing a new type of product. Consequently the main burden in addressing this issue of deceptive selling at the higher inter-professional levels of finance will need to rest on a better education of finance professionals…and perhaps on a reform of the rating agencies.

Rating agencies: moral hazard and irresponsibility

In identifying a key role for the rating agencies in respect of moral failings underpinning the crisis this chapter has only reiterated a theme, which has been widely prevalent since the first explosion of the financial crisis in September 2008. As noted above there are two sorts of moral failing of which they have been accused: moral hazard and negligent incompetence. To address the incompetence the improvement both of education both technical and moral as already suggested for higher level finance professionals in general in the previous paragraph can play a key role here also. Moral hazard questions are rather more difficult to deal with. Since these arise as we saw from the manner in which systems of incentives operate to tempt certain agents to immorality while certainly moral education can help to reduce the temptations for the agents, surely the key and most immediate way to deal with moral hazards is to readjust the relevant incentive system that is causing the problems In the case of the rating agencies this means an adjustment which would reduce the temptation to overrate certain types of junk securities. There have been suggestions that the agencies should be somehow made into state organs, which would therefore have a certain neutrality in relation to private sector issuers of securities and would moreover not be operating under a profit motive, hence would not be under a competitive pressure to overrate certain securities just to secure commissions. There are however two drawbacks with such a suggestion: firstly a significant amount of the securities being rated are government securities of various kinds and so there would be a huge moral hazard present in rating government securities. (To be sure, there is also the difficult question of *which* government would do the ratings?)[21] The second danger is that if public

21 This is actually a rather interesting question because under the current system the three big rating agencies, Standard and Poors, Moodys, and Fitch are all US based even if Fitch is 50% French owned (but Fitch is in any case has much the smallest market share of the three at15%), a fact which by itself must raise big questions about the neutrality and so reliability of the current system. One thing is for sure however: most of the

sector agencies are charged with rating they too could be subject to corruption of their officials by issuers.

In fact – as suggested in an earlier work written with Alek Nowak[22] – the only logical solution to the moral hazard present in the rating agencies is to leave them as independent private sector agencies but to force them to revert to the system whereby they operated before 1973; that is to say to a system whereby the fees of the rating agency are paid not by the originator of the securities being issued but rather by potential investors on demand. Of course, the rating agencies will be up in arms and lobby strongly against any such suggestion and it would require concerted international action to bring about the change (as the agencies could otherwise simply go "offshore" and continue their business as usual). There would be therefore a huge political challenge for our supine politicians but then the rating agencies do not exactly command the moral high ground at present.

Morality and the Regulators: the Wider Challenge of Moral Hazard

A final area of moral failing surrounding the financial crisis which has been mentioned above and has well-rehearsed elsewhere both in scholarly research and in the media has been the huge moral hazard that is present in the role of central banks and financial regulators more generally. On the one hand they are supposed to regulate the financial system with a view to eliminating abuses and failings: yet at the same time they are supposed to act as guarantors of financial stability. In the case of central banks in particular this means being prepared to intervene to bail out banks which may be facing insolvency and resultant runs because of the systemic risks (of a general credit crunch and paralysis of the whole payments system in an economy) which the failure of any one credit giving institution can pose. Of course, the bigger the credit institution, the bigger the systemic risk that is posed: the much touted *too big to fail*, or rather *too big to be allowed to fail*!

Now while it is easy to identify the fairly obvious moral hazard in this (banks and the like can be reckless as they like because, if things go wrong, the central bank and the regulators will bail them out) what is not at all so obvious is what to do about that moral hazard. In fact as long as we have a banking system based on fractional cash reserves it is difficult to see how this moral hazard can be avoided. It is true that recent attempts at *re*-regulation which aim strictly to separate retail

rest of the world would never accept the US government to rate their securities. A UN agency perhaps… unlikely given the politicisation of that body.

22 See O'Sullivan P, Smith M. and Esposito M. (2012), ch. 11.

banking operations from investment baking to some extent address this but they have not eliminated the danger of *retail* banks being reckless (although strict regulation of the retail banking sector can help to achieve this); and there is still always a danger that collapses in the investment banking arms of big financial institutions could translate into a sudden loss of confidence also in the retail banking arms of the same; and such a collapse of confidence, whether justified or not, is all it takes to set off a run and a panic at retail level. Any run on a bank at retail level must require a huge bailout from the central bank or government *by definition* under a fractional reserve banking system.

So an ultimate solution to moral hazard could be the ending of fractional reserve banking at least at retail level. The idea has been discussed[23] and entertained but it would represent a very radical solution to the moral hazard problem. Moreover fractional reserve banking can be defended for its role in the facilitation of investment as banks lend on otherwise sterile funds. But given the long history of credit crunches and financial crises and the damage they wreak when they occur perhaps the time has come serious to consider an ending of fractional reserve banking at least for the retail banking sector. Central banks could far more effectively then exercise their regulatory function, reckless investment banks could be allowed to fail without threat to the whole of the payments system;[24] and governments would not need to be worrying about the huge potential hole in their public finances if they have to get involved in guaranteeing retail bank deposits bailout.[25]

---

23 See for example, the views of Mervyn King, ex-governor of the Bank of England: to the horror of the banking sector he actually suggested the abolition of fractional reserve banking in a well reported speech in 2010 (see report at http://www.economist.com/node/17363435). He is not alone by any means: for example Austrian economists Friedrich von Hayek and Murray Rothbard. Even Otmar Issing who once was chief economist at the ECB has occasionally had his doubts on fractional reserve banking and has flirted "full reserve" banking although in the end he thinks it would be circumvented in the cat and mouse game of the financial system and its regulators. A particularly trenchant critic has been Godfrey Bloom (an MEP): see for example http://www.politics.co.uk/comment-analysis/2014/02/28/comment-don-t-be-fooled-our-economic-woes-haven-t-gone-anywhere.

24 In effect – and with a certain poetic justice – investment banking would be subject entirely to "market discipline"; the higher risk of bankruptcy and failure if overly reckless.

25 The Irish government in particular knows all about this. Ireland's turnaround from a fiscally comfortable country even with budget surpluses to a country with a black hole deficit is entirely accounted for by the government's open guarantee to back all retail bank deposits in Irish banks in the immediate aftermath of the 2008 crisis.

Moral Improvements for the Eurozone in Face of the Sovereign Debt Crisis

In the analysis already presented in this chapter we identified in addition to the general moral failings that underpinned the worldwide financial crisis of 2008 some more specific moral issues of the Eurozone's debt crisis: the Troika morality play, the moral irresponsibility of the politicians who ran up the enormous public sector debts (and of their venal advisors) and the insouciance of many of the buyers of government bonds who paid scant attention to macroeconomic fundamentals.

Borrower recklessness

At a very basic level the Eurozone sovereign debt crisis is about reckless over-borrowing by governments in certain countries with little appreciation of the macro-economic risk of entering the zone of unsustainable debt that arises when governments are forced to borrow ever more as debt matures just to pay interest and principal on existing debt. That is to say a situation arises where the growth of the economy and resulting larger tax receipts are not enough to cover the interest element on past debt: hence not only is the original principal rolled over into further borrowing; with the interest uncovered as well the government borrows even more than the original principal and at that point the debt begins to spiral out of control[26]. When this stage is reached the public sector debt becomes unsustainable in the long run. The antidote to this recklessness once again lies partly in the education both moral and technical of the politicians and their economic advisors: a better understanding of some fairly basic macroeconomics together with an appreciation of the damaging consequences of hyperinflation in particular could help. But given the temptation especially hard to resist for politicians in representative democracies to promise all manner of spending and at the same time tax cuts (hence by definition increasing budget deficits and so borrowing in the first instance) in the run-up to elections it could be argued that it is useful to have in place some kind of constitutional or other regulatory framework to keep the reckless politicians in check especially in representative democracies.[27] Around the world many countries have today given a degree of political independence to

26 If the borrowed funds are coming from the central bank this can degenerate quickly into hyperinflation.

27 Of course, populist dictatorships are subject to exactly the same tendency for politicians to over-borrow so as to curry favour.

their central banks charging the self-same central banks with the goal of maintaining low inflation and currency stability. Central banks can then act as a moral brake on excessive government borrowing provided their governors have real political independence. Within the Eurozone, of course, the European Central Bank has from the outset been politically independent but that has not been deemed to be enough to curb reckless government borrowing in certain states as indeed the sovereign debt crises faced by Greece, Ireland, Spain Portugal and to a lesser extent Italy at certain moments over the past 4 years testify.[28] Hence at the instigation of Germany the Eurozone has introduced first the Stability and Growth pact (1995) and more recently the Fiscal compact (2013). This is not the place to go into the details of the political weaknesses of the Stability and Growth pact which lacked any real regulatory force and which in the end was honoured more in the breach (including Germany in the early 2000s!) than in the observance. The Fiscal Compact which entered into force in 2013 as an intergovernmental treaty for those states that have ratified it has somewhat more regulatory teeth. Like the Maastricht Convergence criteria and the Stability and Growth Pact, the Fiscal Compact requires that each state should enact within its constitutional law framework a provision whereby public sector budget deficits are in the long term to tend to between 0% and 1% of GDP and in no one period should they exceed 3% of GDP. Countries are also expected in the long run to bring their sum total of outstanding public sector debt to 60% or less of GDP. Where countries do not observe these rules other member states of the fiscal compact can bring the errant state before the European Court of Justice that can apply fines and penalties. Also for a country to benefit from funding from the European Stability Mechanism (a kind of Eurozone funding mechanism to provide assistance through special loans in times of financial crisis to member states) it must have implemented the Fiscal Compact ideally into its constitutional law or failing that at least as part of is national laws. There is no doubt that fort those countries who have applied it the Fiscal Compact[29] represents a strong external regulatory discipline on the behaviour of national politicians in terms of public sector borrowing and thereby makes a key contribution to curbing recklessness in borrowing. It also explains, of course, why Euroskeptic politicians are so critical of it: it is a clear EU-level regulatory constraint on national politicians' sovereignty.

---

28 By a sovereign debt crisis here I mean specifically a situation where their governments faced difficulty in placement of their bonds when rolling over past debts at maturity.

29 While the Fiscal Compact has been ratified by all of the 18 Eurozone states many non-Euro states have also ratified it but with varying degrees of commitment.

Lender recklessness: should creditors take more care?

In Streeck's critique of the Troika "morality play" discussed above we noted that just as much as debtors can be morally expected to repay their debts when they can it is also morally incumbent on creditors to pay some attention to whom they are lending in the first place and what may be the chances of default. As we said earlier when dealing with the issues of morality in the selling of complex derivatives, when transactions are occurring between finance professionals at least there must be some role for the *caveat emptor* principle: the person or institution according the credit should be taking care as to what sort of debt they are buying. As above the remedy to this moral failing must lie in the provision of a better education both moral and technical (in terms of economics and finance) to all actors in the financial markets and particularly those operating in the relatively uncharted territory that is the Eurozone. It is after all the world's first ever experiment of a supra-nationally governed shared currency.[30] We also noted already the futility of seeking to regulate in detail derivatives and the whole process of securitisation: not only has securitisation also brought great benefits through greater flexibility and sophistication in financial products, it is in any case virtually impossible to regulate tightly because of the cat and mouse game between finance professionals and regulators. Hence the emphasis needs to be primarily on the decency and the competence of financial market actors, both individual and institutional.

Transference of burden and responsibility for public debt

One of the most disturbing aspects of the morality play identified by Streeck in the Eurozone is the manner in which there has in effect been a gross transference of responsibility for the debacle of the high debt states from the politicians and their venal advisors who contracted the debt in the first place and the populace at large of those states who are now deemed to have the moral responsibility to repay it according to the dominant Troika morality play. This moral failing goes right to the heart of representative democracy and so raises as much questions

---

30 Let us be clear: the gold standard was not supra-nationally governed and was in no real sense a common currency: it was at best a common reserve, horribly limited in physical supply and under the ultimate control of a small coterie of states or private barons. Also the attempted Latin Monetary Union of the 19th century (in Europe) was little more than a system of fixed exchange rates in relation to gold and silver and was strictly intergovernmental in character. Not for nothing did the Economist dub the Euro at its inception "an Awfully Big Adventure"! See *The Economist*, 9 April 1998; available online at http://www.economist.com/node/159442.

of political as of moral philosophy. It also makes resolution considerably more intractable given the nature and prevalence of representative democracies in the world today. The solutions to this moral problem (partly in the nature of a moral hazard) are in principle fairly easy to see but in practice very difficult to implement in representative democracies whose governments claim sovereignty over their national affairs. For example, holding politicians personally accountable in some manner for debts incurred by the state could certainly put a curb on their zeal to borrow recklessly. But unfortunately in a representative democracy that would involve elected politicians enacting not only curbs on their freedom of action but also severe penalties for non-compliance: not very likely I am afraid. Direct democracy can offer a way around the problem insofar as if the people as a whole through a referendum or an assembly enact a public sector spending, taxing and deficit programme for the state, then in the first place the people at large can be held morally liable for the repayment without problems of transference; and precisely because of that they are likely to be a lot more careful about the borrowing than are elected representative politicians. While there are probably many other good reasons besides this one to prefer direct democracy to representative democracy[31] unfortunately such democracy can only work effectively (for simple logistical reasons) in relatively small states and so is unlikely for the foreseeable future to become a prevalent political model: it would involve the break-up into much smaller regional units (cantons and city states) of most of today's sovereign nation states. The world's big nation states in particular are far from ready for that.[32]

---

31 Closeness to the people; much less likely to engage in warfare against other states; much less likely to degenerate into internal civil war; sense of direct involvement for all citizens and so much greater sense of civic responsibility on the part of the majority of citizens and so less crime…

32 Intriguingly however when we look at alternative indicators of social progress such as the Social Progress Index in the top ten performers on social progress in 2013 there are only 2 large states: Australia and Canada. Moreover the top 5 places are taken by small states: New Zealand, Switzerland (a direct democracy!) Iceland, Netherlands, Norway. See http://www.socialprogressimperative.org/data/. The European Union has toyed with and to a small extent institutionalised a radical notion: "Europe of the Regions". See http://cor.europa.eu/en/Pages/home.aspx. If these regions were small enough they could become the nucleus of a direct democracy in the EU. But in these days of Euroskepticism that is perhaps a long way off. Nonetheless the challenge to the European nation states implicit in a Europe of the Regions is a very fundamental one.

Towards a Political Ethics

But if universal direct democracy remains a pipe dream for the moment and if representative democracies are unlikely to enact serious curbs to render their politicians seriously accountable (even if the Fiscal Compact does go in this direction for the Eurozone states) we are for the moment going to have to rely on the encouragement of a greater sense of moral responsibility in the representative politicians we have got. This brings me to conclude the chapter on a theme, which I believe deserves far greater attention than it has hitherto received: the need for *political ethics.* For the past thirty years we have in universities, business schools, assorted think tanks and NGOs been devoting a huge amount of attention to the development of ethics and morality for business: Business Ethics and Company Social Responsibility (CSR). This has been necessary and laudable and by today the fruits of these studies are being truly felt throughout the world. Certain activities in which businesses may have been prepared to engage in the ruthless pursuit of profit without hesitation 30 years ago today are in definite decline. Consider for example environmental awareness in respect of disposal of waste; diversity and non-discrimination in the work place; standards of honesty in advertising… Of course, we are far from perfect in these areas but we have also progressed a long way from the 1980s.

But while all of this attention in terms of both teaching of courses and academic research has been lavished on how to get businesses to be more ethical virtually nothing has been said on the topic of political ethics: getting politicians also to be more morally responsible. The contents of this chapter will have already shown a very fertile field for the application of political ethics (responsibility in respect of the conduct of the public finances). But there are many more fields crying out for the development of moral standards in politics and I will confine myself here to suggestion of but a few. Consider for example the whole question of bribery and corruption in politics. There has been a huge amount of attention paid to the responsibilities of businesses to avoid making all manner of corrupt payments or bribes: rather less attention has been paid to the morality of the high level politicians who accept or even demand big bribes; and who in many cases draft legislation regarding licences precisely with a view to lining their own pockets with bribes to obtain (or to circumvent) the relevant licences.

Conclusions

In representative democracies there is the question of vote buying whether blatant (here is 100; now vote for me) or more subtle (vote for me and there will be a subsidy for your village or a tax break for your industry). And let us be under no illusions: these practices occur in some of the world's most advanced democracies as well as in poor less developed states. How morally acceptable are such practices because in the end democracies will elect he or she who can pay the most rather than he or she who is best fitted for the job. Related to this is the effect of the media on elections in many representative democracies already alluded to earlier in this chapter. Elections have become to a large degree beauty contests and *ad hominem* slagging matches among candidates or propaganda wars among partisan media outlets rather than informed debates on the real issues. Once again how morally responsible is such degeneration of political debate for the politicians and indeed for the media outlets who facilitate it?

I could go on... but it would be inappropriate in this work. Suffice it to say that a key contribution to dealing with a number of the moral failings that we have identified in the financial crisis in general and in the Eurozone's special crisis of sovereign debt could in part be addressed by the initiation of a real study of **Political Ethics**[33] and an encouragement of politicians of all stripes to apply such an ethics in their conduct of public office. This side by side with a parallel education in business ethics for finance professionals and a far more profound technical study of Economics and Finance for all concerned in financial markets could go a long way to resolving many of the issues identified in the course of this chapter.

Bibliography

Blyth M. (2013), *Austerity: the History of a Dangerous Idea*, Oxford: Oxford University Press.

Kling A. (2013), "The Financial Crisis: Moral failure or Cognitive Failure?", *Harvard Journal of law and Public Policy*, Vol. 33, pp. 507–518.

Krugman P. (2013), "How the Case for Austerity Has Crumbled", *New York Review of Books*, 6 June. Available at http://www.nybooks.com/articles/archives/2013/jun/06/how-case-austerity-has-crumbled/.

Mandeville B. (1732), *The Fable of the Bees or Private Vices Public Benefits*, Oxford: Clarendon Press.

O'Sullivan P., Smith M. and *Esposito M.*, (2012), *Business Ethics: a Critical-Aapproach Integrating Ethics Across the Business World* London: Routledge.

33 In capitals: Political Ethics because I believe that it is high time that we recognise such a subject. Not that the suggestion is new: it goes back to Plato's Republic!

Streeck W. (2013), in: Fourcade M, Steiner P, Streeck W. and Woll C. (2013) *Moral Categories in the Financial Crisis,* MaxPo discussion paper 13/1, Paris: Max Planck Sciences Po Centre on Coping with Financial Instability.

Steiner P. (2011), *Les rémunérations obscènes: le scandale des hauts revenus en France*, Paris: La Découverte.

Alojzy Z. Nowak,
Kazimierz Ryć

Crises and World Economy Financialisation

Introduction

If we observe the world today from economic and social points of view, what seems quite striking is, most of all, vast disproportions in terms of income. A couple of years ago, at an international business academy colleagues from Harvard University published the findings of their studies carried out by universities of the US East Coast concerning trends occurring in the contemporary world. This is well illustrated by the following Figure 4.1:

Figure 4.1: Comparative growth rates of distributive shares.

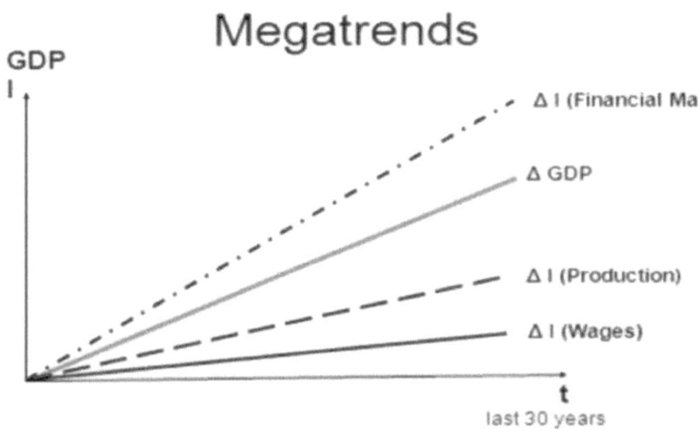

Source: own.

We see how the income looked like, how the change of income from labour evolved, i.e. how wages were shaped world-wide; how income on financial operations in financial markets developed – and they did at a level much above that of the rate of economic growth. By income on financial operations we mean income derived from sale of securities.

This way, as can be seen, the period of the last 30 years saw the formation of quite a serious disparity between income on financial operations and that from production, from labour. In effect, as I dare to argue, partially following my colleagues, but at least partially concluding from my own studies and inquiries, this was one of the key factors responsible for the growth of what we refer to as **financialisation** of the economy.

Accordingly, another observation regarding the modern world, in particular these 30 recent years is the phenomenon of financialisation.

Global Economy Financialisation in Essence

Financialisation may be understood as an increase or a progress or quantitative growth of financial instruments in relation to the gross domestic product. To put it a different way, what we witness is a sort of an absurd situation in which the number of financial instruments in circulation – i.e. beyond the banking system, in hands of businesses and households, – is much higher that might have been expected from actual needs of the GDP size. If we take a look at figures, at present the world's GDP amounts to, or better oscillates, roughly at the level of 65 trillion American Dollars. This is contemporary world's GDP and it should be added that the share of two groups of countries: the United States and the European Union (28 countries) in generation of this GDP is at the level of about 60%. At present the EU as a whole ranks at the leading position while the United States follow at number two.

The amount of financial instruments in circulation, instead, including monetary resources, i.e. securities, credits for both non-financial and financial sectors and obligatory reserves amount, according to Joseph Stiglitz, a Nobel Prize winner in economy in 2004 and Professor at the Columbia University, but also according to estimates of the Financial Times and Deutsche Bundesbank – a level of ca. 600–650 trillions of American Dollars.[1] This very relation of these financial instruments, the amount of financial resources in hands of businesses, to the GDP is what we call financialisation.

This ratio, therefore, looks like 10 to 1 assuming some approximation. This means that in today's world we have more or less ten times more financial resources than is really needed to buy goods and services the same world generates. As we noticed: present the world's GDP oscillates, roughly at the level of 65 trillion American Dollars, and the amount of financial instruments in circulation is estimated at level of ca. 600–650 trillion.

Such a first-glance impression is in clear opposition to what we are all experiencing. If things look this way, then we should enjoy an excess of financial

1 Data presented by Professor J. Stiglitz during his visit at University of Warsaw, Poland, 2011.

resources while the feeling we do experience is quite an opposite – that we suffer from a deficit of these resources so there must be simply not enough of them. Where is the problem, then, or how to align these diverging perspectives? Unfortunately, the problem in the contemporary world consists in the fact that a considerable part of the financial resources in question are, with some simplification, non-economic duds – we call them toxic assets. It is worthwhile here to quote two American professors: Paul Krugman and Joseph Stiglitz, who – together with their teams – carried out sets of comprehensive calculations. What may be concluded in the light of their findings as well as from analyses prepared for Deutsche Bundesbank and for The Financial Times, is that toxic assets account for about 30 % of total assets in various parts of the world. These are financial assets nobody wants to acquire and nobody really knows what to do with them. Since this is, roughly, 180–185 trillion US$ we are speaking about enormous sums. Actually, this is more than today's world GDP. See Figure 4.2:

Figure 4.2: Financial assets: GDP.

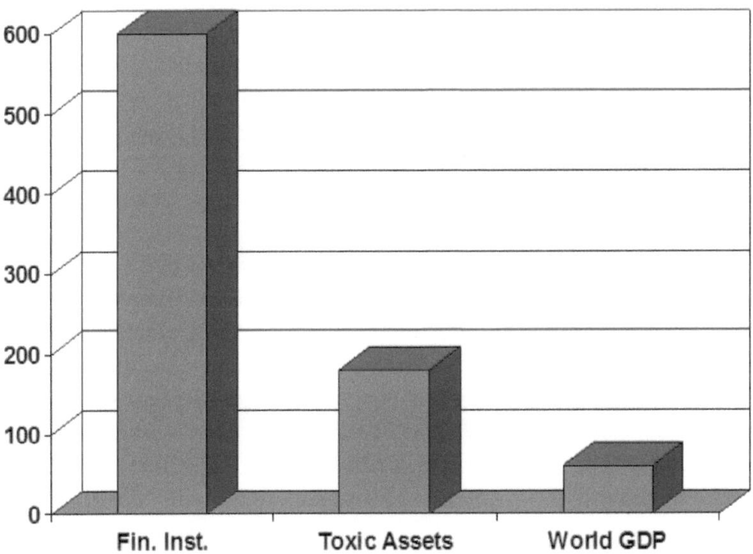

Source: own.

Moral Dimension of the Financial Crisis

The obvious question now is: where these assets originated from?

Firstly, it should be emphasised that it would be wrong to consider the problems in question without taking into account the moral and ethical sphere. These moral failings have been dealt with in detail already in Chapter 3. Accusations against many institutions aren't just fabricated. We all know about the case of Lehmann Brothers, a powerful New York-based bank, as we do cases of various grand financial corporations (many of them in the insurance sector) that used to generate financial instruments despite being perfectly aware these were quite worthless. They put them in the market and encouraged the broader public to acquire the same, supporting their incentives with highly favourable opinions voiced by three American rating agencies: Standard&Poor's, Moody's, and Fitch.

What was found out was that in order to meet the banks' needs, the agencies guaranteed these instruments with triple A's, thus confirming their thorough financial reliability. Actually, even the most risky mortgage investments were given best rates, as were many other financial instruments that proved worth nothing after the speculation bubble blew up. The US Congressional Commission that examined the reasons of the financial disaster of 2008 concluded that mistakes made by rating agencies belonged to the most serious engines driving the mechanism of financial meltdown.[2] There is a fabulous film entitled the *Inside Job* available on YouTube, where one of the Presidents of the great rating agencies tries to explain why his institution confirmed total financial credibility of another institution on Monday or Tuesday, giving it a triple A, while just a couple of days later the same was found at the verge of bankruptcy. His explanation is more or less: "It was just an opinion."

Just an opinion, then, and he did not even find it noteworthy that it was American taxpayers who paid dearly for that. Students learning business, wherever they study, should be reminded time and time again that there is nothing to replace their own reason, their own independent consideration and judgment about the reality. Anything else may be bought and what is bought is always going to bear some risk and when it comes to opinions, bias. Warren Buffett fits well as an example to follow in this respect. When asked whether in need of advisers, he replies that he only invests in what he understands. And when he fails to understand some things regarding

2 The Financial Crisis Inquiry Commission (FCIC) set up by the US Congress and President to investigate the causes of the financial crisis, concluded that the failures of the Big Three rating agencies were "essential cogs in the wheel of financial destruction" and "key enablers of the financial meltdown" (2011).

business-related decisions, he simply does not invest. What's the use of advisers, then? The answer seems only too clear.

Perhaps there's just one other thing worthy of mention here, remembering that this is not a chapter dealing exclusively with finance. The financial instruments the value of which was estimated at about 650 trillion American Dollars number are of more or less one thousand distinct types. They are very different and complex. Now, to quote a belief Professor Stiglitz expressed during a meeting in the National Bank of Poland, it would be extremely misleading to imagine that those who acquired financial instruments in the market over the period of last 30–40 years really understood what they were buying. They bought because they saw others buying. And as soon as the duds, the toxic assets, found their way into institutions, they often implied their quick bankruptcy, but, importantly, with the investors being the ones who suffered the cost of the disaster.

This is a huge problem in the contemporary world. Why the problem of contemporary world? Because, despite the fact we are living in the world of reforming deregulating economies we call market-based economies, the society – in other words, we as the citizens – still have the feeling there must be somebody over us who bears responsibility. And the first answer that comes to mind, especially as we speak about the US, is that the responsibility rests with the ruling ones, with the state administration. In broader terms, and reaching beyond the American context, it is the state that should take responsibility for us. However, the state often seems quite uncertain about how to behave as there are several sometimes divergent viewpoints upon the economy in it, stemming from different economic schools; and one school advocates in fact eliminating the regulatory role of the state in the economy.

The schools in question may be divided into two groups. One is known as proponents of absolutely free market – these are those representing the "Chicago school," sometimes dubbed in Europe ultrliberalism or market fundamentalism; while others belong to the "post- Keynesian school" which assumes more or less active involvement of state in the economy and in Europe are known as advocates of the social market economy. Whilst the former ones ask the following questions: was there anybody to force the institutions to generate the financial instruments? The answer is no, nobody made them do it, they were created independently. And then, did anybody order the buyers to purchase financial instruments appearing in the market? And again the answer is no – nobody made them buy. Very well, therefore – say proponents of the Chicago school – let the businesses fall down so that the market clears itself automatically. After all, the investors were supposed to be conscious about choices they made. If they want to operate in the market they should be prepared to the task, they should carry out insightful analyses and only purchase healthy financial instruments.

The other group, that representing the post-Keynesian school, perceives this in a different way. They say: well, indeed you – ultraliberals– are right to a certain extent, but the real trouble is that as the financial institutions infected with toxic assets fall down, their bankruptcy is going to entail a chain reaction of many other businesses tumbling down as well in the real economy sphere, causing increased unemployment. And as unemployment increases, then who will stand up to bear responsibility for people, families and households affected?

There were times when such problems were solved through wars, declared, among other things, in order to stimulate some sectors of economy ad to reduce unemployment by conscripting the unemployed and, of course, by casualties. Personally, I am a tremendous opponent of this solution. Nowadays we are all aware of massive tragedies wars were bringing but we also know that in the long run they also often result in decline of several sectors of economy and really increase the unemployment.

There is yet another problem faced by the modern world. The vast majority of state budgets are almost empty, as all admissible standards on expenses exceeding revenues have been violated. At the same time, the state with its budget remains responsible for four fundamental spheres of public life. This was aptly described by a remote cousin of a prominent Polish political economist Michał Kalecki, a British economist Anatole Kaletsky, in his book entitled *Capitalism 4.0*. Michał Kalecki, an extraordinary economist himself, perhaps a potential Nobel Prize winner should he not have died prematurely, was a competitor of John Maynard Keynes – the father of state intervention concept. Both Michał once and his cousin Anatole nowadays have pointed out what the state, i.e. the government in particular, should be responsible for: most of all for education, for health care and health safety, for social insurance and for civil security. Today, under a crisis situation, with public finance and many financial institutions on the edge of bankruptcy, the state, struggling with its high budgetary deficit, has to decide what to take care of, i.e. to redefine its real priorities.

As a result at present in face of the global crisis many states face a stark choice, whether to involve themselves more in bailing out the financial sector of the economy or in supporting the society's broader interests. In most countries governments seem to prefer to bail out the financial sector, thus channelling their limited means and capabilities to save the economy. At the same time the protection or support to many social needs is postponed for some better time. This is what we are witnessing, to a considerable degree, in Poland, in the European Union and in the US and Canada as news abounds with talk about restricting the state spending on education, health care, pension funds and even on defence.

Questions About The Nature of State and Economy

State governments have to make decisions, make choices in what to invest. That's how a fundamental political problem arises: if they give up the protection of the four above-mentioned basic sectors, a day will come when societies are going to ask: what's the use of state, is it any good at all? We have already had this sort of experience; and we end up witnessing social unrest, even in a number of rather wealthy countries. On the other hand, we cannot forget the experiences of the so-called real socialism either and what that taught us: indeed, entire states were going bankrupt in consequence of having taken excessive and often unreasonable welfare obligations while having an inefficient economy.

All this sums up to a very complicated global situation from financial and economic points of view. It seems next to impossible to clearly, unhesitatingly formulate the path to follow. In the past and really until quite recently it was easier to find a solution as the ultimate objective of the market economy was clearly defined, as was the road market economy was meant to take to achieve it.

Recent decades saw a so-called Washington Consensus (see Chapter 1 above) prevailing in the theory of economy. Rather than proceeding just from pure academic considerations, it also stemmed from some real tendencies occurring in the process of globalisation. The megatrends in global economy included, in particular, deregulation, liberalisation and privatisation.

These three principal trends were supplemented by the process of economic integration in many geographic areas of the world. The example of the European Union is perhaps the most illustrative in this context. All it takes to heal the world economy was sought in the three above-mentioned ideas. Whatever there was wrong, whatever crisis was experienced in the economy, liberalisation, deregulation and privatisation were called to lend a helping hand. Such solutions were approved by both the World Bank and the International Monetary Fund. After the communist system had fallen down, an ultraliberal doctrine, restricting the role of state in the economy and diminishing the role played by the public sector, became a crucial element of systemic transformation in many countries, including especially in emerging economies. And when the crisis came –it arrived quite unexpectedly right from the country from which the ideas of the Washington Consensus originate and where they were implemented with much enthusiasm- the United States.

The global financial crisis of the years 2007–2009, unanticipated both in its scale and range, became the turning point that led to a scrutiny of the concepts included in the Washington consensus. Its consequences reach far beyond its initial period. Some theoretic assumptions made in economic theories based upon a belief in built-in self-regulating and repairing mechanisms in free market economy failed to stand up to this scrutiny. Worse still, deprived of such regulation mechanisms, the system began to produce all sorts of degeneration and dysfunctions. It was especially mistakes and distortions appearing in financial markets that became particularly painful and destructive for the real economy as well as for regular citizens. The cost of the turbulence was mainly borne by common American taxpayers.

Is the Chinese Model of Any Use?

In the course of delivering lectures to Chinese students (both in continental China and in Taiwan) during discussions about global market or financial institutions, they would often ask: what to do, then, under such conditions? "We were neither liberalised nor deregulated. We weren't privatised, either, and look – ours is a flourishing economy whilst yours, the Western one, is most obviously diseased," they would add. It is extremely difficult to come up with a clear-cut answer to this. Any potential answer depends, to a significant extent, on the particular university one graduated from and on the views that have tended to predominate in the teaching in that institution. As a result there can be very diverging interpretations of similar economic phenomena; and, of course, one has to admit there are political beliefs influencing this issue.

In Poland, indeed in the entire European Union or perhaps in the whole world we are arguing about what was the reason behind the crisis of today's capitalism. Is this lack of a clear answer to the question a problem? We think it is. What is of the utmost importance for us ere in Europe is how to overcome the crisis in the Euro Area, one that emerged in the wake of the global financial crisis. For many European countries the process of recovery from recession raised social issues too, rather than merely economic challenges. Since the consequences of the financial crisis conveyed from the United States also exposed serious weaknesses with potentially drastic social consequences inherent in mechanisms of Euro Area operation. We debate about how to make the Euro area more efficient and competitive as we see the advantages it brings. At the same time we would like to underline that the Euro Area crisis should not be mistaken for any crisis of Euro as a currency – actually, the latter has fared quite soundly. The key problem we perceive is one of asymmetry in public indebtedness as among Euro area states and its solution requires at least in part a restoration of the situation when the European Union was permeated by the spirit of community and solidarity. This used to give an invaluable impulse towards European integration and towards impressive overcoming of any remaining negative heritage of the World War 2. Poland is most interested in the success of the project known as the European Union and the Euro Area. It was largely thanks to it that we have managed to make up for historically determined economic and civil underdevelopment –a process that is admittedly ongoing.

The Crisis from Poland's Viewpoint

Today Poland enjoys much more dynamic and competitive economy than ever before. Still, there are problems emerging on the way toward further healthy progress. Here we come back to issues concerning financial systems. The world used to rely upon two different financial systems, one being known as complementary or German-Japanese system while another was the Anglo-Saxon one. The former one was primarily based upon the banking system: support was given for the economy through credits and loans made by banks and other financial institutions. The latter one, i.e. Anglo-Saxon, mainly relied on invisible hand of the market – on financial institutions, deregulated financial markets, and above all stock exchanges. The direction of changes seemed rather clear: towards the Anglo-Saxon system. Poland has also rebuilt its economy on the basis of this system's assumptions, as it really seemed the most efficient one. This was manifested establishment of the Warsaw Stock Exchange, the key objective of which was and still is to acquire and supply loanable funds (capital) to companies while it was left to the market to evaluate the value and efficacy of individual investments.

Today we already know that, unfortunately, the system never came to operate really well, either in Poland or anywhere else in the world. Market deregulation on a global scale has resulted in the emergence of profound divisions, to a sense of flagrant injustice and, worse still, to inefficient use of loan able funds (capital). And so most of debate going on in the world today is really about how to align the two systems, doing it at regulatory level, how to enact common regulation, to introduce means of common control over the financial system. Milton Friedman, the late American economist who was an unyielding supporter of financial institutions' independence and of the free market, near the end of his life observed that there's no such thing as "free breakfast included." According to him, there's a price to pay for everything. And just before he died, so late in his career that hardly anybody listened to him any more, he wrote an essay, arguing that if we afford any financial system total independence, it will begin to live its own life – will begin to operate as the KGB did in the Soviet Union. And that's where a problem appears about whether it is still an organisation within a state or rather a state within a state. Unfortunately, in a certain sense this is the very nature of financialisation. It perturbs the rules that are supposed to apply in the free *competitive* market to a serious extent.

How, then, to find a way out of that trap of financialisation and avoid the many problems it entails? Answers are aplenty and there are several schools to support them. We believe that the strategies for improvement of competitiveness and for increasing the rate of economic and social progress should include a new vision in the area of economic policy in which the state regains a key regulatory role but perhaps in new and innovative ways. Some role for the state, active but still defined within certain limits is not only not going to do damage, in fact it will help in recovering from, let us admit this, a very complex and socially dramatic economic situation in many countries; it will also restore to the state its rightful role under the social contract.

Western Economies' Competitiveness: on the Wane or Not?

In Europe we perceive how the key economies of the West grow weaker and weaker, competition-wise. The process tips the scales more and more towards countries of Asia. Whilst the US and some Euro Area economies still manage to feature high levels of innovation and capabilities of adaptation, nonetheless their advantage in these areas is visibly on the wane.

What is really threatening is that the hitherto-prevailing ethos of a consumption society, based upon the three mainstays of arduous work, higher savings rate and durable capital accumulation, becomes seriously undermined. After all, it's also thanks to that ethos that the foundations of today's advanced capitalist states were laid down, including significant levels of welfare and social service.

The work ethic ceases is no longer considered an absolute priority. Factors, which detrimentally contribute to this situation, include, among other things, a growing belief that any additional effort is no longer justified or no longer rewarded with appropriate financial gratification, so its sense becomes doubtful. Indeed, the above-mentioned degenerations in financial markets had an extremely negative impact upon social awareness in the areas of ethics and morality. People have grown increasingly convinced that income earned with earnest work remains absolutely out of proportion to that derived from playing the stock market or involving in all sorts of speculative tricks. Disillusion and cynicism are as a result rampant.

Finally, we are facing a dangerous crisis of authority of government and rule of law. Until quite recently it was commonly believed that liberal democracy, rule of law and civil society were the best remedies to any temptation of political destabilisation. However, the last financial crisis gave strongly contrary signals with plentiful examples of either regulatory inefficacy or even partial responsibility of political authorities for the conditions of the state and its principal institutions including institutions which seemed to get entirely out of control, thus provoking social protest on a massive scale, contesting the authority of those in power and the very foundations of legal order.

Conclusions

This is how the future of the most developed part of the world finds itself at a dramatic parting of the ways in respect of economic policies and economic ideology. We in the European Union know very well that each crisis in the past ended up consolidating it. However whether the same will hold true on the global scale remains an open question.

Bibliography

Ferguson N. (2010), "Czy kres cywilizacji Zachodu?" (A Decline of Western Civilisation?), *EUROPA*.

Ferguson N. (2010), "Kolos. Cena amerykańskiego imperium" (Colossus. The Price of the American Empire), Warsaw: Wydawnictwo Sprawy Polityczne.

Kenen P. B. (1995), *Economic and monetary union in Europe: Moving beyond Maastricht*, England: Cambridge University Press.

Krugman P. (2008), The Return of Depression Economics and the Crisis of 2008, USA, W.W. Norton&Company Inc., December.

Krugman, P. (2011), "Can Europe Be Saved?", *New York Times Magazine*.

Nowak, A.Z., Shachmurove Y. (2012), "End of Euro Area?", in: *Understanding Global Economy. National and Regional Studies*, Wyd. Naukowe WZ UW.

Nowak A. Z., Ryć_K. (2010), "Out of Crises-But How?", in: *Global Economy. In Search for Solutions to Stabilize the Global Economy*, Vol. 5: M. Baliamoune-Lutz, A.Z. Nowak, J.Steagall (eds.), University of Warsaw, Faculty of Management Publishing, Coggin College of Business, University of North Florida, Warsaw-Jacksonville.

Nowak A. Z. (2007), *European Economic Integration: Chances and Challenges*, Warszawa: Wyd. Naukowe Wydziału Zarządzania UW.

Stiglitz J. E. (2009), "Capitalistic Fools", *Vanity Fair*.

Stiglitz J.E., (2012), *The Price of Inequality: How Today's Divided Society Endangers Our Future*, W. W. Norton & Company (first published 4 June 2011).

Alojzy Z. Nowak

Crisis and Innovation

Introduction

When asked whether the present economic crisis is already on the wane, experts are vague. Some believe that extensive interventions launched by final borrowers (i.e. governments and central banks) have managed to control further escalation of loss of liquidity suffered by regular commercial and financial entities (commercial banks, investment funds, insurance funds, etc.), and that this has brought more optimism into the real economy which should soon translate into more solid economic growth and consistent, if slow-paced, process of recovery from the crisis. Others, instead, point out that, firstly, due to the volume and diversity of financial resources, including toxic assets that remain in circulation, the crisis has in fact only been slowed down a little and that the worst is still to come. Secondly, apart from the USA and some Asian countries, we still face the problem of deteriorating consumer confidence, restricted trust in the future, contradicting strategies for development of global economy as well as that of leading countries and economic/political groups, and, finally, the problem – still observable – of undermined moral principles and lack of ethics in business.

A New Type of Crises

It seems that this fundamental discordance of views upon the future of the global economy stems from the fact that the present crisis is not like the previous cases of economic downturns. Thousands of detailed and often incompatible pieces of information, coming from many countries, actually blur rather than clear the picture of transformation occurring in the global economy. What we have to deal with is a mix of positive and negative information, potentially leading to wrong conclusions. In many countries, financial markets increasingly seem to influence if not dictate the actions taken by political and economic rulers. Nonetheless, possible scenàrios for the global economy's recovery from the present slow-down assume the following:[1]

1 Taplin R., Nowak A.Z, (eds.) (2010), "The financial crises, intellectual property and prospects for recovery. The case of Poland and Central and Eastern Europe", in: *Intel-*

- that a need will emerge at the level of businesses, to recreate their aging productive capacities also at the end of the downturn stage of the classic business cycle. In effect as the cycle bottoms out demand grows up – on the one hand for investment goods such as machines, equipment, new technologies and, on the other hand, this also fosters inventory renewal or shift. The process is slow but it may already be observed in real economy. This is especially evident in the USA or in several Asian countries, China in particular. Hopefully, more and more distinct signals of economic stimulation there precede an improvement of a climate for investment in the entire global economy.
- that it will become possible to implement innovations created or disclosed during the stage of downturn. Usually, a crisis is also a period when universities and research institutions increase their activities, often subsidised from either state or local budgets so that they can absorb jobless youth and raise their skills. As experience teaches us, this process, combined with a growth in business competitiveness, both of enterprises and their employees, results in increased tendency to innovate and launch state-of-the art technologies.[2]

At the same time, we observe how individual governments undertake all sorts of actions in order to overcome the economic stagnation and its consequences and to give new impulse for development in the area of real economy. Traditional methods of recovering from the crisis, undertaken by governments, include, on the one hand, budgetary and fiscal discipline, restricted public spending, raised taxes, but a diametrically opposed and contradictory policy concentrates on stimulating the economy, relaxing the fiscal regime and undertaking actions that aim to increase consumption and to reduce unemployment. What may be observed during a crisis is that some governments reach further than just for standard actions and either increase or at least give up restricting public spending on servicing the needs of elderly population in such areas as biomedicine, health care or social welfare, because it is in development of these fields that they look for potential sources from which new, prospective products or innovative technologies might emerge.

The experience gathered so far also seems to confirm that both strategies of anti-crisis action mentioned above are meant to yield positive results over a

---

lectual Property, Innovation and Management in Emerging Economies, London-New York: Routledge.

2 Nowak Alojzy Z., Ryć Kazimierz (2010), "Out of Crises-But How?", in: *Global Economy. In Search for Solutions to Stabilize the Global Economy*, Volume 5, M. Baliamoune Lutz, A.Z. Nowak, J. Steagall (eds.), University of Warsaw, Faculty of Management Publishing, Coggin College of Business, University of North Florida, Warsaw-Jacksonville.

medium-term perspective. It seems that in the long run consistent efforts to raise competitiveness and productivity of a given economy is the key to achieve a more steady economic development.

Accordingly, innovations become, especially during a crisis:

- a driving force of contemporary economy,
- vital modernisation-promoting factor which increases economic efficiency,
- a factor that lays down foundations for solid and durable economic growth, reinforces the economic potential, and
- a factor that exerts crucial influence not only upon development of businesses, but upon standards of consumers' lives as well.

That's why governments that choose this development model, aim to:

- Extend the area of knowledge-based economy and services,
- Implement a system of education in which priority is given to creativity and new skills creation,
- Reform universities so that they are more strictly related to needs and challenges of local and global economy and with laying down healthy foundations for releasing the potential intellectual capital,
- Support public education where electronic media, Internet and E-learning are capable of playing a vital role in propagating innovative attitudes,
- Create the legal and institutional framework for sound and efficient innovation and government policies friendly to entrepreneurship.

Key Tendencies in Innovation Policies

Due to complexity, cost and risk involved in the process of innovation, the state becomes an important actor in creation of systemic conditions favouring the emergence of new products and business models. Although the role of state as regards these issues is uncontested, still the key to increase of competitiveness and market advantage should be sought in commercial and financial entities themselves and in their approach to innovation.

Today, it is not hard to name the key tendencies in their innovation policies:

1. *Shift from the previous model of creating innovation policy*, based upon a single company, towards one based on collaboration between a number of companies operating in complementary areas of entrepreneurship. It becomes more and more popular to set up new technology clusters or consortia whose cooperation, along with similar scientific or technological levels, also involves better

recognition of a given market local market with its intricacies, including its cultural aspect.

2. *The region increasingly becomes the arena of interaction necessary for modernisation processes to emerge.* Peculiarities and specific potential of a given region allow reduction of the risk involved in innovation, favour the absorption of various segments of knowledge, and open up a room for interactive learning and expertise exchange[3].
3. *SMEs are going to enjoy an ever increasing share in innovation* because it is not only the level of research spending that acts as their principal driver, but it is also their creativity and the ability to exploit a high level of development of science which may be used by individuals and relatively minor groups. Hence the growing importance of innovative family businesses in the market.
4. As a result of an increasing complexity and risk involved in innovation, *relationships between various entities, reaching beyond regular market relations,* are going to grow more and more precious. This will include relations held with universities, research labs, and providers of consultancy and technological services.
5. A concept of *demand-based approach to innovation* becomes a significant method of implementing innovation, oriented at creation of new ideas and solutions.[4] It is based on better cognition and understanding of both evident and hidden consumer demands, expectations and needs. This concept is put into practice through establishment of effective mechanisms of acquiring and exploiting information gathered from consumers as well as – quite often, in fact – by using their ideas or even ready solutions.
6. *Innovation-oriented activities of businesses in 21st Century,* rather than just maximization of profit, is going to mean businesses increasingly oriented to serving specific human needs, variable over time. These expectations may in particular be met by small and medium-sized enterprises. Therefore, new dynamics may be expected in development of areas in which the following will play significant roles:

3 Oleksiuk Adam (2012), *Uwarunkowania i mechanizmy tworzenia innowacji jako czynniki rozwoju gospodarczego* (*Pre-conditions and Mechanisms for Creating Innovation as Factors of Economic Development*), Olsztyn: University of Warmia and Mazury Publishing, p. 317.

4 PARP (2012), "Dlaczego warto wykorzystywać popytowe podejście do tworzenia innowacji? Wnioski ze spotkań Klubu Innowacyjnych Przedsiębiorstw" (Why Is It Worthwhile to use demand-based approach to innovation? Conclusions from meetings of the Innovative Entrepreneurs Club), Warsaw, Poland.

- Green technologies,
- Medical technologies,
- Information technologies,
- Biotechnologies and Nanotechnology.

7. *Cultural factors, traditions, high level of organisational culture and models of economic development* are going to gain an even stronger influence upon the level of innovativeness of businesses and economies.

Innovation Policy in the USA and Japan

The experiences of two very different countries, the USA and Japan, concerning the level and nature of innovation enable one to argue that there are no ready-made, identical recipes for achieving the principal driving forces, on which success of innovation potential depends. The two countries often feature different conditions and mechanisms for creating innovation as factors of economic development.

In the case of the **USA** the following factors are important:

- Americans are interested in achieving success and taking business risk;
- Bankruptcies are also perceived as positive events and seen as one's new business experience and an opportunity to heal the company.
- Protection of intellectual property has been regarded as one of the foundations for development since the establishment of the United States (1776). The first patent was awarded in the USA as early as 1790.
- Tax system favours innovation.
- Foundations are established at both federal and state level to support entrepreneurship and innovation.
- Extensive investments (both private and public) in R&D, in particular in information technologies, nanotechnology, biotechnology, are supported by technological universities.
- It is quite common for small and medium-sized enterprises to become initiators of entrepreneurship development and of high-risk business.

In **Japan**, by contrast with the United States, the following factors influence innovation success to a major extent:

- *Collectivist culture* in which superior importance of a group than of an individual has been emphasised for centuries and belonging to networks of social ties is seen by members of the society as a source of identification and sense of safety, provided among other things by relationship between an individual and a corporation.[5]

- *Kaizen*, i.e. the perfection of work done, has been a key term in the Japanese model of management. It creates an atmosphere in which companies may solve their inner problems avoiding major conflicts. What counts is little improvements done without disturbing the social status quo. Adaptability, team work, close attention to detail and continuous process of small adjustments and incremental innovations sum up to perfect enrichment and supplement the process of proper innovation.
- *Partnership* between large companies and SMEs is often not only based upon economic premises and a propensity to maximise profit, but also on the omnipresent spirit of cooperation and mutual trust.
- *The government supports and initiates creation of scientific consortia*, horizontal cooperation networks, clusters, etc.
- In 2010 Japan ranked first in the world with the number of 295.315 patents applied for domestically.

The Japanese, by virtue of the above-mentioned cultural background, peculiar solutions, and their approach to searching new technologies, are able to offer products featuring perfect level of manufacturing quality and it is not by chance that they enjoy a long-standing reputation for being among the very leaders in all sorts of innovation rankings. Interestingly, other Asian countries, including Singapore, Hong Kong or China also secure top places in this competition.

Table 5.1: Presents the ranking of the world's 10 most powerful production computers in 2011

Rank in 2011	Year of production	Manufacturer	Site	Country	Computer performance PFLOPS
1	2011	K computer Fujitsu	Riken Advanced Institute For Computational Science, Kobe	Japan	10.510
2	2010	Tianhe-1A NUDT	National Supercomputing Center, Tianjin	China	2.566
3	2009	Jaguar Cray	Oak Ridge National Laboratory	USA	1.759

5 Hofstede, G. (2000), *Cultures and Organizations. Software of the Mind*, Warsaw: PWE.

Rank in 2011	Year of production	Manufacturer	Site	Country	Computer performance PFLOPS
4	2010	Nabulae Dawning	National Supercomputing Center Shenzhen	China	1.271
5	2010	Tsubame NEC/ HP	GSIC, Center, Tokyo Institute of Technology	Japan	1.192
6	2011	Cielo Cray	Los Alamos National Laboratory, Los Alamos	USA	1.110
7	2011	Plejades SGI	NASA Ames Research Center, Mountain View	USA	1.088
8	2010	Hooper Cray	National Energy Research Scientific Computing Center, Berkeley	USA	1.054
9	2010	Tera 100 Bull	Comissariat à l'Énergie Atomique (CEA), Bruyères-le-Châtel	France	1.050
10	2009	Roadrunner IBM	Los Alamos National Laboratory, Los Alamos	USA	1.042

Source: Top 500 Supercomputer Sites.

Summing up this part, it seems undeniable that high level of innovativeness in a given country largely depends on whether the government, various sectors of industry and services, and scientific and academic circles sum up to create a system of complementary relationships. The search for new, common sources of knowledge and technology should be accompanied by appropriate institutional and legal infrastructure.

Creation of new, original knowledge and its dissemination isn't possible unless substantial outlays are made, both public and private, in R&D, as a GDP percentage. Experience to date indicates a firm relationship between R&D spending, the number of patents, especially those applied for abroad, and share of high-technology goods in a country's exports.

Table 5.2: Innovation ratios in selected countries in 2010

Item	Public outlays on R&D (as %of GDP)	Number of patents applied for abroad	Country	Number of patents applied for domestically	Share of high technology goods in total export (%)
1	4.86	5387	Israel	1387	23
2	3.44	53.281	Japan	295.315	20
3	2.82	231.194	USA	224,912	23
4	–	85.477	China	229.096	31
5	2.72	11.724	Germany	47.859	16
6	3.75	306	Sweden	2549	17
7	3.46	127	Finland	1806	18
8	2.02	1809	France	14.295	23
9	1.88	6480	United Kingdom	15.985	23
10	2.72	131	Denmark	1518	18
11	1.63	53	Netherlands	908	24
12	2.66	292	Austria	2263	11
13	1.47	92	Czech Republic	789	16
14	1.34	207	Spain	3596	5
15	1.18	903	Italy	8814	8
16	1.03	12.966	Russia	25.589	9
17	0.90	68	Croatia	250	12
18	0.61	242	Poland	2899	5
19	0.59	37	Romania	1054	10
20	0.47	63	Slovakia	176	5

Source: The Author's own calculation basing on: World Development Indicators, http//data.worldbank.org/indicator/TX.VAL.TECH.MF.SZ/countries (downloaded on 2013.02.07).

Table 5.2 shows there is some relationship between the level of public spending on R&D measured as GDP percentage and a share of high technology goods in export.

Conclusions

These days, such countries as Netherlands, Israel, Japan, United States, Germany, France, or United Kingdom are leaders in the market of exported advanced technology goods and most often these are also goods patented abroad. This group also includes China, actually in first position with 31 per cent share of high-tech goods in exports. This goes to confirm what seems very likely anyway, that China is becoming a country exporting more and more sophisticated technologies, and this is not only the case to the so-called Third World countries, but in Asia, USA and Europe as well.

It is evident how China has embarked on the shift from the stage based upon copying foreign solutions towards expanding their presence in global markets through offering goods and services increasingly based upon its own original and innovative solutions. And the other way round, countries ranked near the bottom end of Table 5.2, such as Poland, Romania or Slovakia, also serve well to illustrate how a low level (as GDP percentage) of public spending on research translates into a very weak percentage share of high technology goods in their export.

The Table 5.2 also shows very clearly why it was Budapest in Hungary rather than Wroclaw in Poland that was chosen as a seat of the European Institute of Innovation & Technology. The share of high technology goods in Hungarian export in 2010 amounted to lofty 26 per cent of the country's total export, while in Poland it was as little as 5 per cent.

If Poland suffered the consequences of the global crisis to a relatively lesser extent, it was also – and paradoxically – thanks to relative technological underdevelopment of its banking sector and relatively minor share in operations concluded in global financial markets. As far as innovativeness is concerned, Poland has nowadays faced challenges related with the shift from the present stage of development to the next one in which the search for now sources of knowledge and technology prevails, as well as of possibilities of their practical application. The awareness that innovations have become – as mentioned before – a driving force for the contemporary economy, and that they act as factor promoting modernisation and increase in efficiency, that they reinforce the economic potential and, via exports, lay down foundations for long-term economic growth, becomes more and more widespread today. It applies everywhere, including Central and Eastern Europe.

Bibliography

Edvinsson L. (2012), "Universal Networking, Intellectual Capitalin", in *European Integration Process in the Regional and Global Settings*, E. Latoszek, I. Kotowska, A.Z. Nowak, A. Stępniak (eds.), Warsaw: University of Warsaw, Faculty of Management Publishing.

Hall B. H., Mairesse J. (2009), *Measuring Corporate R&D Returns. Presentation to the Knowledge for Growth Expert Group*, Directorate General for Research, European Commission, Brussels.

Hiroka M. (2006), *Innovation Dynamism and Economic Growth. A Non-Liner Perspective*, Edward Elgar, Cheltenham, England.

Hofstede G. (2000), *Kultury i organizacje; zaprogramowanie umysłu, (Cultures and Organisations. Software of the Mind)*, Warsaw: PWE.

Klincewicz K. (2011), *Dyfuzja Innowacji (Innovation Diffusion)*, Warsaw: University of Warsaw, Faculty of Management Publishing.

Kołodko G. (2012), "Ekonomia kryzysu, czy kryzys ekonomii" (Economy of Crisis or the Crisis of Economy), in: *Kryzys i co dalej? (Crisis... and What Next?)*, I. Lichniak (ed.), Warsaw: Warsaw School of Economic Publishing.

Legrain Ph. (2010), *Aftershock: Reshaping the World Economy after Crisis*, London: Little Brown.

Nowak A.Z., Ryć K. (2010), "Out ofCcrises-But How?", in: *Global Economy. In Search for Solutions to Stabilize the Global Economy*, Vol. 5, M. Baliamoune-Lutz, A.Z. Nowak, J.Steagall (eds.), University of Warsaw, Faculty of Management Publishing, Coggin College of Business, University of North Florida, Warsaw-Jacksonville.

OECD (2010), *The OECD Innovation strategy. Getting a Head Start on Tomorrow, htpp://www.oecd.org/innovation/strategy/*, Paris.

Oleksiuk A. (2012), *Uwarunkowania i mechanizmy tworzenia innowacji jako czynniki rozwoju gospodarczego* (Pre-conditions and mechanisms for creating innovation as factors of economic development), Olsztyn: University of Warmia and Mazury publishing.

Oliveira M. G., Rozenfeld H. (2010), "Integrating Technology Roadmapping and Portfolio Management at the Front-end of New Product Development", *Technological Forcasting& Social Change*, No. 77, p. 65.

Polish Agency for Enterprise Development: PARP (2012), *Dlaczego warto wykorzystywać popytowe podejście do tworzenia innowacji? Wnioski ze spotkań Klubu Innowacyjnych Przedsiębiorstw (Why Is It Worthwhile to Use Demand-Based Approach to Innovation? Conclusions from Meetings of the Innovative Entrepreneurs Club)*, Warsaw, Poland.

Prahalad C. K., Krishnan M. S. (2010), *Nowa era innowacji (The New Age of Innovation: Driving Co-Created Value Through Global Networks)*, Warsaw: PWN.

Taplin R, Nowak A.Z., (eds.) (2010), "The financial Crises, Intellectual Property and Prospects for Recovery. The Case of Poland and Central and Eastern Europe", in: *Intellectual Property, Innovation and Management in Emerging Economies*, London-New York: Routledge.

Tidd J., Bessant J. (2011), *Zarządzanie innowacjami (Managing the Innovations)*, WoltersKluwer Publishing: Poland.

Part III

Grzegorz Tchorek[1]

How to Fix the Euro Area? Poison and Remedy: The Roots of the Crisis and New Institutional Solutions[2]

Introduction

The objectives of this chapter relate to three main issues: firstly, identification of the main weaknesses of the euro area mechanisms which led to the crisis; secondly, an assessment of the introduced and proposed reforms; and thirdly, a proposal for the optimum institutional model of the euro area in the future.

The main findings from a review of the literature indicate that the euro introduction was based on incorrect assumptions, which led to real and nominal divergence between countries despite expected convergence. Moreover, the economic and financial crisis exposed the degree to which the euro area was an incomplete monetary union due to insufficient stabilisation instruments and a low level of solidarity between countries.

The new institutional arrangements introduced in the EU are a big step towards strengthening current and establishing new mechanisms forming the necessary fiscal, economic and financial pillars of the monetary union. However, the progress and quality of their implementation is conditioned by a lot of factors. The main risks, which can undermine the effectiveness of the reforms, are connected with the fact that they are related to a broad set of economic and political aspects and demand giving up national competences which need to be delegated to the UE level.

The proposed model of European cooperation of a "hub and spoke" type means that the single currency is based on the power of institutions rather than on the power of sovereignty. It can be considered as a transitional form of integration between the decentralised monetary union that prevailed before the crisis, and a

1 The expressed views reflect the opinion of the author, not that of the institution for which he works.

2 The article is extended version of the article "Źródła kryzysu a nowe rozwiązania instytucjonalne w strefie euro" (Roots of the Crisis and the New Institutional Arrangements in the Euro Area), published in *Finanse*, No. 1(7), 2014, a journal edited by Komitet Nauk o Finansach PAN.

highly centralised model of full political union, considered (by many at least) as the ultimate goal for the UE, and especially the euro area.

Theoretical Foundations of the Euro Area Structure and the Sources of the Crisis

The main arguments in favour of the euro area establishment included the elimination of exchange rate risk and transaction costs resulting from dealing with a number of different currencies. Monetary integration was expected to entail significant transformations in both financial dimension and real economies of the euro area.

Firstly, the common currency was intended to stabilise inflation expectations, which, in the 1970s and 1980s, constituted the principal source of macroeconomic instability, also causing by serious exchange rate volatility, frequent devaluations and inadequate fiscal discipline.

Secondly, lessons learnt from the debt crisis of the 1980s in Latin America, resulting from excessive foreign debt of the countries, and the currency crisis of Autumn 1992s suggested that the elimination of exchange rate risk might reduce the macroeconomic instability and country risk resulting from currency speculation and the threat of bankruptcy related with the so-called *original sin*.[3]

Thirdly, a large and integrated financial market, covered by common currency and monetary policy, was meant to facilitate access to a deep and diversified financial system and to stimulate processes of real convergence.

Fourthly, it was assumed that integrated financial markets would act as mechanisms absorbing asymmetric shocks – *risk sharing channel*.[4] (See Table 6.1.).

In the real economy, the euro adoption was meant to increase the efficiency of the monetary unions' economic system through better price transparency, stimulated competition and increased trade and investments,[5] as well as more incentives for

---

3 The so-called *original sin* may affect developing countries, which borrow money in foreign currencies, thus exposing themselves to the risk of losing their ability to service their debt as a result of a profound devaluation/depreciation of national currency. Eichengreen. B., Hausmann R., Panizza U., *Currency Mismatches, Debt Intolerance and Original Sin: Why They Are Not the Same and Why it Matters*, NBER Working Paper No. 10036, 2003.

4 Kalemi–Ozkan S., Sorensen B.E, Yosha O., "Regional Integration, Industrial Specialization and the Asymmetry of Shocks across Regions", *Journal of International Economics*, 2001.

5 Mongelli F. P., De Grauwe P., "Endogenities of Optimum Currency Areas: What brings Countries Sharing a Single Currency Closer together?", ECB Working Paper No. 468, 2005.

structural reforms.[6] Therefore, there appeared expectations that even if a country was not ready to participate in the euro area, it would be easier for it to fulfil the conditions of Optimum Currency Area (OCA) as a member of the monetary union – endogeneity of the OCA.[7] Convergence of income levels, just as a correlation of business cycles, was also expected as a result of increased trade.

Table 6.1: Macroeconomic assumptions and experiences of the euro area

Prior to the crisis it was assumed that:	**In the wake of the crisis it occurred that:**
Elimination of exchange rate risk	
– would reduce the macroeconomic risk by stabilizing the inflation expectations and increase the efficiency of market-based mechanisms through integration of national markets into a Single Market and elimination of *home bias*, – would reduce the risk of currency crisis and bankruptcy due to the absence of exchange rate risk and elimination of the so-called original sin;	– might lead to other types of risks and market dysfunctions, for example excessive debt and credit booms, – might lead to susceptibility to contagion and speculation in financial market segments other than the foreign exchange market, as well as market fragmentation – might increase the risk of bankruptcy due to inability to monetize debt;
Structural convergence	
– would proceed as a result of intensified trade and synchronization of business cycles: endogeneity of the OCA criteria, – would be stimulated by structural reforms through market discipline and inability to use currency devaluation as a competitiveness tool (known as the TINA argument, *i.e.* There Is No Alternative);	– had not really happened. Instead, divergence had appeared, due to: – significant disparities in term of GDP per capita and economic structures among economies when the euro area was established, – pro–cyclical macroeconomic policy and boom and bust phenomena, – lack of flexibility of economic structures and capability of meeting the Maastricht criteria in a sustainable way, – lack of structural policy to boost competitiveness;

6 Duval R., Elmeskov J., "The effects of EMU on structural reforms in labour and product markets", ECB Working Paper No. 596, 2006.

7 Frankel J. A., Rose A., "The Endogeneity of the Optimum Currency Area Criterion", *The Economic Journal*, 108/1998, pp. 1009–1025.

Financial markets integration	
- would stimulate economic growth, - would facilitate financing of balance of payment deficits, - would alleviate shocks through the so-called risk - sharing mechanism, - would uniform the mechanisms of monetary policy transmission.	- had contributed to the boom and bust phenomenon, thus abruptly increasing divergence, - had acted as both generator and accelerator of shock due to the inadequate and fragmented financial supervision and the *sudden stop and reversal* phenomenon as well as reemergence of the *home bias*, - might, in the absence of institutional integration, lead to financial fragmentation and dysfunctions in the mechanism of monetary policy transmission.

Source: G. Tchorek, Źródła kryzysu a nowe rozwiązania instytucjonalne w strefie euro, Finanse 1 (7) 2014.

Assessments made until 2008 indicated that many of the above-mentioned benefits of the monetary integration had become a reality. Nonetheless, the crisis over the years 2008–2012 revealed many weaknesses of the euro area mechanisms. The crisis also contributed to the deepening of many dysfunctions of the common currency system. In evaluating a period of almost fifteen years of the euro area functioning, it may be argued that **the monetary integration** failed to fulfil many expectations. In a number of fields, mechanisms of the euro area have to be reformed or even new institutions should be established.

Firstly, experiences of the euro area countries (as well as other EU member states maintaining fixed exchange rates, such as Baltic countries or Bulgaria) suggest that elimination of exchange rate risk may indeed improve microeconomic efficiency of the economy (lower interest rates and costs of capital as well as capital flows from wealthy to poor countries). However, from a macroeconomic point of view, greater availability of cheap money may cause the risk of excessive debt in the private sector leading to of boom and bust cycle phenomena. The integration of financial markets, spurred by elimination of exchange rate risk and common monetary policy in place of national policies, contributed to an abrupt reduction of interest rates, improved access to financing and soaring cross-border capital flows. Increasing differentials in national inflation rates made common monetary policy pro-cyclical because of negative real interest rates and led to excessive debt in the private sector and accumulation of macroeconomic imbalances.

Secondly, in the absence of crisis management mechanisms, an abrupt outflow of private capital from the Southern countries of the euro area resulted in contagion effect because of speculation in financial markets. In consequence of the private sector debt, dependence on wholesale short-term **financing sources and exposition to American toxic assets, the euro area was affected by a banking crisis. Due to the enormous size of national banking sectors** (several times bigger than GDP), the banking crisis had a severe impact on the financial systems as well as on national sovereignties. National budgets suffered from the requirement to nationalise the collapsing **financial institutions or to act as guarantees for them. (Ireland was the clearest instance of this as the government undertook at the height of the crisis to guarantee entirely all bank deposits in Irish banks).** Liquidity problems experienced by the governments of member states then contributed to the insolvency crisis. A growing speculation as to the risk of the euro area break-up, on the other hand, spurred sudden stops and reversals in capital inflows and a balance of payment crisis.[8]

The lack of institutional stabilising mechanisms, including the effective absence of the lender of last resort function for the governments of the Euro area from a central bank, revealed that the risk of the individual euro area countries collapse might be more serious than in the case of a country with its own currency and therefore its own central bank. The elimination of exchange rate risk failed to eliminate the risk of the original sin, so it did not protect the euro area member states from the risk of speculation against any given economy and, in particular, against its government's debt or from the contagion effects. Despite the absence of national currencies, speculation still became a problem in the government bond and derivative markets.[9] Accordingly, financial markets which – as originally assumed – were meant to absorb asymmetric shocks, became their source themselves. Because of downgrading credit ratings, serious turbulence in government securities' markets, banking crisis and freezing of wholesale money markets, the mechanism of monetary policy transmission was seriously disturbed. Financial markets underwent the fragmentation process, which led to increasing differentiation of long-term interest rates and cost of credit for the private sector in the situation of historically the lowest ECB's nominal interest rate.

---

8 Bijlsma M., Valee S., *The creation of the euro area financial safety nets*, Bruegel Working Paper 2012/09, 2012.

9 S. De Santis, "The Euro Area Sovereing Crisis. Save Haven, Credit Ratings Agencies and the Spread of the Fever from Greece, Ireland and Portugal", ECB Working Paper No. 1419, 2012; Arghyrou M.G., Kontonikas A., "The EMU Sovereign-Debt Crisis: Fundamentals, Expectation and Contagion", European Commission Economic Papers No. 436, 2011.

The data presented in Figure 6.1 suggest that financial markets integration did not really support the process of structural transformation in the Southern euro area economies and that, at the same time, it may have been an important source of macroeconomic imbalances (see Figure 6.2). In the cases of Greece, Portugal and Italy, the credit was directed towards private consumption and homeowner mortgages. In Ireland and Spain, the credit was also targeted at companies but it was largely allocated to the non-tradable goods sector. Moreover, the currency integration contributed to the worsening of the structure of foreign capital inflow, shifting it towards debt financing (bank and market debts), with a diminished role played by FDI and equity financing. It exposed the peripheral countries to the financial shock after Lehman collapse in 2008 to a greater extent than the countries financed more by equity flows.

Figure 6.1: Financing structure of the chosen euro area economies.

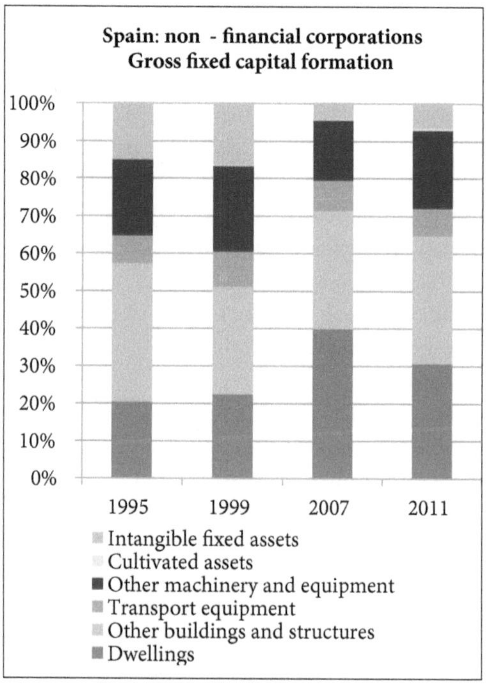

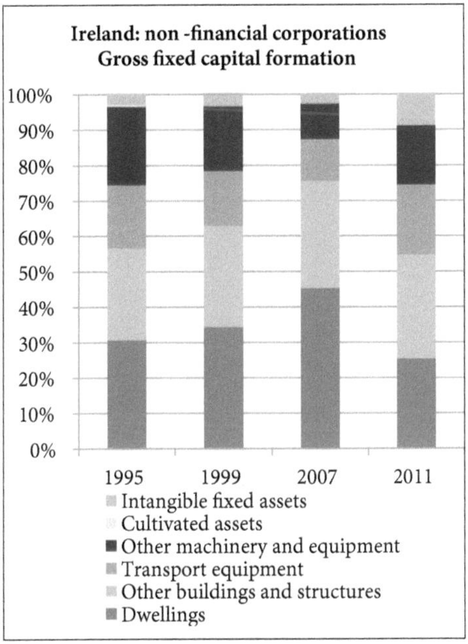
Ireland: non -financial corporations
Gross fixed capital formation
100%
90%
80%
70%
60%
50%
40%
30%
20%
10%
0%
1995
1999
2007
2011
Intangible fixed assets
Cultivated assets
Other machinery and equipment
Transport equipment
Other buildings and structures
Dwellings

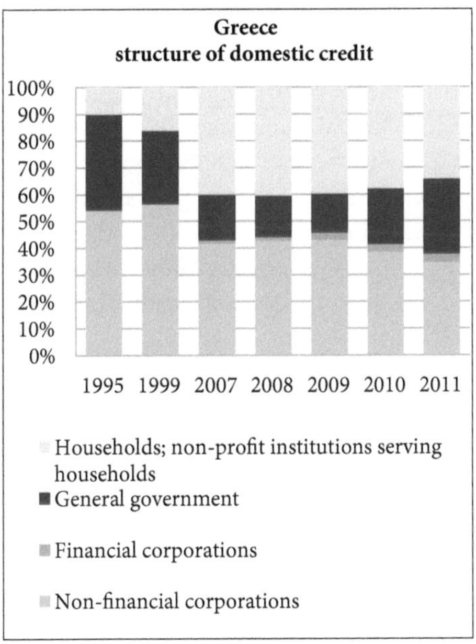
Greece
structure of domestic credit
100%
90%
80%
70%
60%
50%
40%
30%
20%
10%
0%
1995
1999
2007
2008
2009
2010
2011
Households; non-profit institutions serving households
General government
Financial corporations
Non-financial corporations

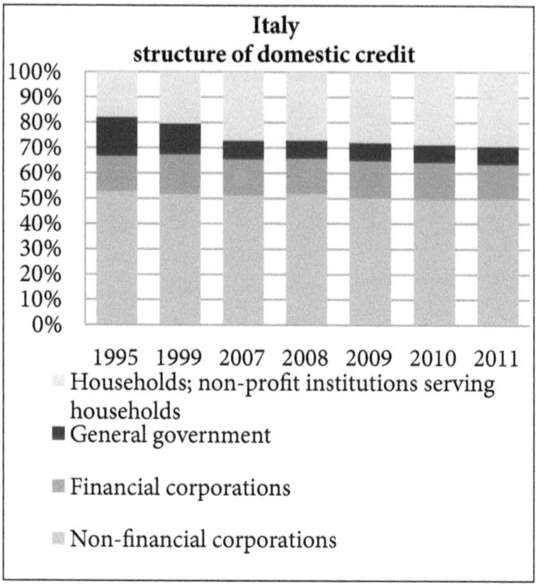

Source: Own calculation, based on the Eurostat data.

Thirdly, mechanisms were missing to eliminate structural differences between countries, as were instruments preventing and correcting the macroeconomic imbalances. Divergences largely manifested themselves as a result of the price competitiveness loss by some member states' economies, accompanied by inflexible labour and goods markets. This led to appreciation of real f exchange rates,[10] which was caused by increasing inflationary differentials, stemming from, among other things, consumption and investment booms. Simultaneous wage pressure in the services sector triggered the shift of production structure towards non-tradable sectors, lowering export market shares.

Fourthly, the impact of the euro on trade appeared to be lower than expected. The original outlook was based on the assumption of a strong influence of exchange rate risk elimination over trade and business cycles correlation. This phenomenon was usually called the *endogeneity of the optimum currency area criteria*. Experiences of initial years of the monetary union indicate that the *euro effect*, i.e. additional trade volume by virtue of the adoption of the common

10 Despite the lack of nominal exchange rates between countries of the monetary union, real exchange rates can still fluctuate as a measure of relative prices and costs changes.

currency, amounted to around 2–5%. This means that the impact of the euro was weaker than expected and weaker than the influence of other determinants, such as ongoing globalisation and inclusion of emerging economies with low labour costs (like China, Central and Eastern European Countries) in international trade, changes in raw material prices, appreciation of the euro from 2001 to 2008, and reallocation of foreign investment outside the euro area because of higher GDP growth of the global economy than in the euro area.[11]

Fifthly, in terms of the influence of the euro adoption over FDI flows, the early expectations were also greater than investment actually made. According to initial evaluations, the common currency had a positive impact on the FDI flows both within and beyond the euro area.[12] Petroulas argues that the introduction of the euro could have contributed to an increased flow of FDI between the euro area countries as well as to increased outflows of FDI from the euro area to third countries.[13] On the other hand, Taylor comes up with less encouraging conclusions.[14] He observes that, excluding the flows to Luxembourg from the group of the analysed countries, changes in the FDI flows between the euro area countries were below average for all the countries worldwide. As regards significance of the euro introduction for FDI, studies by Flam and Nordstrom indicate that common currency cannot be considered as a decisive factor. They suggest that the single market effect may be more important for FDI flows[15]. Dinga and Dingova also seem quite far from confirming the influence of the euro on FDI[16]. What they notice, instead, is the significance of the EU membership as a factor stimulating the FDI flows.

In the context of these observations, it seems worthwhile to consider the examples of Greece and Italy, i.e. countries in which no major growth of direct

---

11 Mroczek W., "Wpływ wprowadzenia euro na stopień otwartości i zmiany strukturalne w handlu krajów strefy euro" (Influence of the Euro Implementation on the Openness and Structural Changes in Trade of the Euro Area Countries), in: *Raport na temat pełnego uczestnictwa Rzeczypospolitej Polskiej w trzecim etapie Unii Gospodarczej i Walutowej*, 2009.

12 Sousa J., Lochard J., "Does the single currency affect FDI?", *The Scandinavian Journal of Economics*, Volume 113, Issue 3, page 553–578, 2011.

13 Petroulas P., "The Effect of the Euro on Foreign Direct Investment", *European Economic Review* 51, 2007.

14 Taylor C., "Foreign Direct Investment and the Euro: the First Five Years", *Cambridge Journal of Economics*, Vol. 32, 2008.

15 Flam H., Nordström H., *The Euro Impact on FDI Revisited and Revised*, Institute for International Economic Studies, Stockholm University, Swedish National Board of Trade, 2008.

16 Dinga M., Dingova V., "Currency Union and Investment Flows: Estimating the Euro Effect on FDI", IES Working Paper: 25/2011.

investment inflow was recorded in the wake of the euro adoption – see Figure 6.2. Investment attractiveness of these countries was largely limited by poor institutional quality (complex unfriendly legislation, malfunctioning administration, etc.) and low international competitiveness. One peripheral country, which, unlike the two other, absorbed relatively much investment, is Portugal. Nonetheless, sectoral structure of FDI inflows shows bias toward non-tradable sector, mainly services targeted at market penetration rather than export activities.

As we see from the example of Portugal, in addition to the scale of FDI inflows, their structure should also be taken into account.[17] Empirical studies suggest that the composition of FDI inflow in the euro area countries, as well as the EU non-euro area countries, could determine divergent levels of labour productivity and economic competitiveness, and magnitude of external imbalances.[18] In the case of the monetary union, Northern countries mainly attracted FDI in more productive industries while Southern ones absorbed more investment in non-tradable sectors.

Figure 6.2: Foreign Direct Investment in the euro area.

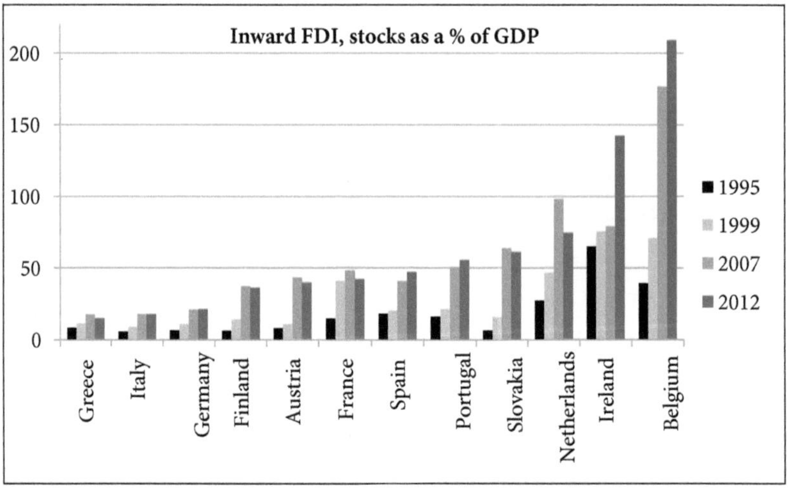

Source: UNCTAD.

17 Christodoulakis N., Sarantides V., "External Asymmetries in the Euro Area and the Role of Foreign Direct Investment", Bank of Greece, 2011.

18 Mitra P., "Capital Flows to EU New Member States: Does Sector Destination Matter?", IMF, WP, 2011, Kinoshita Y., "Sectoral Composition of Foreign Direct Investment and External Vulnerability in Eastern Europe", IMF, Working Paper, 2011.

The above experiences indicate that instead of an expected convergence, following an initial period of positive tendencies, serious divergences appeared among the euro area countries. A number of studies emphasise a growing divergence, especially over the last couple of years preceding the crisis. Lewhad, who examined changes in production, investment and consumption in both sub-periods, i.e. over the years 1991–1998 and 1999–2010, distinguished a group of "central" countries including Belgium, France, Germany, Italy, Finland and Netherlands and "peripheral" countries of the Euro Area (Greece, Ireland, Portugal and Spain).[19] He points to greater synchronisation of cycles in the earlier period in both groups of countries. Nevertheless, following the introduction of the common currency, the synchronisation increased only in the central countries while the peripheral countries recorded its decline. The author explains closer economic and financial ties within the former group with increasing significance of the global factors (trade and financial flows), which are more important in the central than peripheral countries. Sinn *et al.* confirm that capital inflow to the peripheral countries accelerated the economic growth; however, in northern countries, which exported capital, investment rates shrank as a result of economic stagnation.[20] Miles *et al.*, in examining correlation of the cycle between four peripheral economies (Greece, Spain, Portugal, and Ireland) and the central ones, i.e. Germany and France, do not observe more intensive synchronisation in the case of the two former ones and confirm a decrease in case of Ireland and Greece. As they evaluate changes in synchronisation between the euro area centre and three economies of the European Economic Area not belonging to the euro area (namely Denmark, Switzerland, and Sweden), the authors do not note lower synchronisation in the two former cases and observe higher synchronisation in the case of Sweden. These observations indicate that growing importance of the "central" countries actually confirms Krugman's hypothesis concerning production concentration as a result of monetary integration and undermines Rose's hypothesis of endogeneity.[21]

19 Lehwald S., "Has the Euro Changed Business Cycle Synchronization? Evidence from the Core and the Periphery", Ifo Working Paper No. 122, 2012.

20 Sinn H. W., Buchen T., Wollmershäuser T., *Trade Imbalances – Causes, Consequences and Policy Measures*: Ifo's Statement for the Camdessus Commission. CESifo Forum, 12(1), 2011.

21 Contrary to Rose's assumptions, Krugman indicated, giving the example of the USA, that a common currency may lead to agglomeration of production and to increased differences among business cycles in individual areas (for more details, see Mongelli P., 2002).

Weaknesses of the Maastricht Treaty

There is no doubt that the crisis in the euro area is a part of the global crisis. However, the above-mentioned deficiencies of the euro area functioning also had their roots in a flawed institutional structure established under the Maastricht Treaty. Most of all, the rules of the Treaty focused on fiscal stability limited to such issues as the level of budget deficit, loose coordination of member states' macroeconomic policies and price stability as the fundamental objective for the central bank. It was assumed that there would be no need to have crisis mechanisms in place because the Treaty rules were meant to prevent any crisis – see Table 6.2.

Table 6.2: Assumptions of the Maastricht Treaty and experiences of the euro area

Prior to the crisis it was assumed that:	**In the wake of the crisis it occurred that:**
Fiscal Policy	
– would be stable and credible thanks to market discipline and to the Treaty rules containing the budget deficit limit of 3% and the *no-bail out clause;*	– had been ineffective in building anti-cyclical buffer and preventing excessive public debt; – had not been accompanied by financial market discipline (interest-free ride), which was aggravated by the problem of *zero risk free weight;*
Economic and Structural Policy	
– would be coordinated at the European level through non-binding coordination instruments (Open Method of Coordination), – would be *a matter of common interest;*	– requires more advanced and stricter instruments of coordination and alignment of common goals in order to prevent negative spillover effects, – requires elimination of incentives for the *beggar thy neighbor policy;*
Monetary Policy	
– should be focused on narrowly understood price stability;	– should be extended to include the function of ensuring the **financial** stability, including the macro-prudential policy, – should ensure the lender of last resort function;

Prior to the crisis it was assumed that:	In the wake of the crisis it occurred that:
Crisis Management Mechanisms	
– would not be necessary because the Treaty rules prevented fiscal and balance of payment crises;	– should constitute an indispensable element of the financial safety nets in the euro area, since the lack of them undermined the trust in the stability and future of the monetary union project, – should have been established *ex ante*, because the process of their establishment during the crisis inevitably entailed a great deal of political dispute;
Division of the EU into the Euro Area countries and Non-Euro Area countries	
– would not be a real problem since the Maastricht Treaty assumed that all the EU member states would eventually become the euro area members too.	– constituted a serious barrier to the process of agreeing upon new institutional solutions, and led to the risk of a two-speed Europe.

Source: G. Tchorek, Źródła kryzysu a nowe rozwiązania instytucjonalne w strefie euro, Finanse 1 (7) 2014.

Fiscal policy

According to the assumptions of the OCA theory, the monetary union should be accompanied by an integrated fiscal policy in the form of a common budget ready to initiate transfers between individual countries in reaction to asymmetric shocks. The importance of such an instrument had already been signalled by, among others, Ingram as early as in 1959 or McDoughall in 1977. As a result of the lack of either social or political consensus on the establishment of a common budget, fiscal rules defined under the Maastricht Treaty emerged as a substitute of the common budget. On the one hand, their aim was to facilitate the implementation of an anti-cyclical fiscal policy, the role of which is indeed increasing once national monetary policies have been given up. On the other hand, the introduction of fiscal rules in member states' policies was to reduce the risk of excessive debt of individual countries at the cost of the other ones (moral hazard). Protective measures against these threats were included in the Excessive Deficit Procedure (EDP), specifying the threshold of 3% budget deficit in relation to GDP as well as the *no-bail out clause* prohibiting provision of "financial rescue." According to the latter one, neither European institutions nor member states should have to bear responsibility for other member states' debt. However, these instruments bringing discipline into fiscal policy failed to prove effective, for the reasons discussed below.

Firstly, this was caused by a simple failure of the European institutions in enforcing the provisions of the Stability and Growth Pact (SGP). The first serious weakness of the SGP appeared in 2003 when the EU Council did not adopt the European Commission recommendations concerning the sanctions against two largest countries exceeding the 3% limit, i.e. France and...Germany! Indeed, throughout the history of the SGP, not a single fine has ever been imposed on any EU member state, despite the rules being violated many times.

Secondly, this was a consequence of the lack of member states' ownership of or commitment to fiscal rules defined at the European level.[22] The problem of violating the rules not only concerned the above-mentioned largest countries (in 1999–2008, Germany and France infringed the 3% deficit criterion five and four times, respectively), but, most of all, Greece (which actually never met the criterion from the time of its accession to the euro area until 2008), Portugal and Italy (the limit of 3% of GDP for budgetary deficit being exceeded six times), as well as some EU member states not belonging to the euro area.

Thirdly, financial markets' discipline weakened in the euro area and in the whole global financial system. The elimination of exchange rate risk premium in the euro area, which was perceived as a factor eliminating the risk for a given country and in particular for its government bonds, removed differences between the levels of long-term interest rates. The relationship between the quality of fiscal policy and long-term interest rates were weakened as well. Moreover, financial markets did not attach much importance to the no-bail out clause. This resulted from the assumption that should any member state face bankruptcy threat, its debt would be bailed out by other member states because of their close economic and financial ties.[23] Finally, financial market failure also stemmed from global factors, in particular – after 2003 – from low interest rates in the main global financial centres, increasing global capital (loanable funds) supply as a result of saving glut, low risk aversion and search for yield.

---

22 Filipek A.K., Schreiber T., *The Stability and Growth Pact: Past Performance and Future Reforms*, Working Papers 97, Department of Economics, College of William and Mary Foreign Relations (ECFR), 2010.

23 Gianviti F., Krueger A. O., Pisani-Fery J., Sapir A., von Hagen J., *A European Mechanism For Sovereign Debt Crisis Resolution: A Proposal*, Bruegel, 2010.

Economic policy

The euro area's official name is the Economic and Monetary Union. However, the EMU lacked common economic policy and, as evidenced by the crisis, it has not even become a properly functioning monetary union so far. Instead, one centralised monetary policy run by the ECB was accompanied by entirely independent national fiscal and macroeconomic policies. In the area of national macroeconomic and structural policies, the Broad Economic Policy Guidelines were meant to play the role of a coordination tool. Unfortunately, this instrument was not legally binding upon member states and non-compliance was not regarded as a violation of law.[24] What the Treaty actually required was only that countries, while running their economic policies, regard them as a matter of common interest by taking the goals and priorities defined at the EU level into account. Therefore, the Open Method of Coordination failed to provide a sufficiently effective instrument to ensure that the euro area's (and, in fact, the entire EU's) competitiveness and stability is treated as a common good.[25] In consequence, the economic policies as conducted by many of the nation states were leading to instability of the euro area economies (booms in real estate markets in both Ireland and Spain) as well as those of the other EU member states (such as expansion of Scandinavian banking over Baltic countries, which also contributed to the emergence of bubbles). The literature also points out that the institutional model of the EU left vast room for running a *beggar thy neighbour policy.*[26]

Monetary policy

Based on the experiences of inflation in the 1970s and early 1980s, inflation was considered the crucial risk for stable macroeconomic environment. In the face of general increase of central banks' independence since the early 1990s, a measure

24 Oręziak L., *Finanse Unii Europejskiej* (*Finances of the European Union*), Warsaw: PWN, 2004.

25 Tchorek G., "Czy można odnosić korzyści z integracji walutowej?" (Possibility of Benefiting from Monetary Integration), in: *Mechanizmy funkcjonowania strefy euro* (*Mechanism of the Functioning of Eurozone*), Owsiak S. (ed.), Cracow: Wyd. Krakowska Szkoła Biznesu Uniwersytetu Ekonomicznego w Krakowie, 2013.

26 Laski K., Podkaminer L., "The Basic Paradigms of EU Economic Policy-Making Need to Be Managed", *Cambridge Journal of Economics*, 36(1), 2012; Vernengo M., Perez-Caldentey E., "The Euro Imbalances and Financial Deregulation: A Post-Keynesian Interpretation of the European Debt Crisis", Working Paper No. 702, Levy Economics Institute, 2012.

that became more and more popular was the inflation targeting strategy with an evident focus on price stability as the only objective for the central bank. Thus, stabilisation of inflation came to be seen as the key guarantee of macroeconomic stability. Unfortunately, this approach failed to take into account the challenges of counteracting speculative bubbles and financial systems' instability.

Capital outflow from the euro area peripheral countries as well as the lack of crisis management mechanisms exposed another weakness, namely the absence in effect of a lender of last resort (LOLR) for the national governments. As the contagion effect was spreading, in the face of missing crisis management mechanisms and speculation about the euro area break-up, expectations appeared with respect to the ECB perhaps assuming such a role. This was especially important as, with no LOLR role played by the ECB, countries were issuing debt in a currency (*the Euro*), which remained beyond their control. A further consequence was that liquidity crisis led to insolvency crisis. The EFSF (European Financial Stability Facility) and then the ESM (European Stability Mechanism: initiated January 2013), which were meant to perform the role of a substitute for the LOLR function, proved ineffective due to financial restrictions that, as such, are not relevant for the central bank in its role of the lender of last resort.

The problem of balance of payment crisis and lack of stabilisation mechanisms

Before the crisis, the balance of payment imbalances in the euro area member states was not regarded as serious[27]. This was manifested in the Treaty regulations stating that the euro area member states could not use the balance of payments assistance mechanism (Article 143 TFEU). This approach resulted from the assumption that among states using the same currency there is no balance of payments problem in the classical sense (any more than there can be a balance of payments problem between member states of a federal state, between say Baden Wurtembug and Hesse in Germany); rather it was assumed that capital flows from central to peripheral countries would ultimately be balanced by tightening trade, capital and investment relations.[28] Catching up countries were borrowing capital which was intended to stimulate income convergence and enable the borrowers

27 Merler S., Pisani-Ferry J., *Sudden Stops in the Eeuro Area*, Bruegel Policy Contribution, 12, 2012.

28 Blanchard O., Giavazzi F., "Current Account Deficits in the Euro Area. The End of the Feldstein Horioka Puzzle?", NBER Working Papers 8120, National Bureau of Economic Research, 2002.

to pay it back in the future. Integrated financial markets were expected to fund the imbalances within the monetary union, as theorised by Ingram as early as in 1972. Moreover, the balance of payments of the euro area as a whole was close to zero or even slightly positive so any imbalances in individual member states were seen as no reason for concern.

However, the balance of payment crisis appeared as a result of banking and fiscal crises. The lack of assistance mechanisms or their provisional nature caused an outflow of capital from peripheral countries. Instead of contributing to depreciation of respective currencies, this phenomenon resulted in the fleeing private capital being replaced with public resources provided by the IMF – EU assistance programs as well as capital transfers within the Eurosystem through TARGET2. In terms of liquidity, the sudden stop is effectively mitigated by the internal payment system of the ECB and national central banks of the euro area countries.[29] However, still there are no systemic mechanisms for alleviating the balance of payment crisis in terms of solvency – see Table 6.3.

Table 6.3: Typology of crises and remedies undertaken in the euro area

Crisis/actions	**Liquidity mechanisms**	**Solvency**
Banking	Government guarantees, unconventiosnal monetary policy actions – SMP, LTRO	Recapitalization by governments
Fiscal	EFSF, ESM, IMF	ESM, private sector restructuring
Balance of payments	Extraordinary support for liquidity	No proposals

Source: M. Bijlsma, S. Valee, The creation of the euro area financial safety nets, Bruegel Working Paper 2012/09, 2012.

The legal structure of the common currency did not foresee a necessity to counteract any liquidity or solvency problems. Accordingly, the euro area system was not equipped with any formal crisis management mechanisms. The lack of clear crisis management rules raised country risk and contributed to a significant increase in bond yields (that is interest rate coupons on government bonds). Thereby, through growing **financing costs, it increased the risk of individual countries going bankrupt. As a result, the euro area actually appeared to be a group of**

29 Bijlsma M., Valee S., *The Creation of the Euro Area Financial Safety Nets*, Bruegel Working Paper 2012/09, 2012.

countries bound by fixed exchange rates, rather than a complete monetary union. What we experienced in the face of the crisis was the return of *home bias* and the actual recurrence of the exchange rate risk, which could have potentially materialised in case of the euro area break-up (*redenomination risk*).

The EU fragmentation: deepening of the division into euro area and non-euro area countries

The designers of the Maastricht Treaty assumed that the EU member states would automatically become euro area members. Thus, they failed to foresee legal problems stemming from the formation of three groups of the EU countries: those belonging to the euro area, countries with a permanent derogation (Denmark, the United Kingdom) and those with a transitional derogation (the remaining EU member states). Prior to the crisis, the problem was not particularly onerous. Relatively fast economic growth, increasing trade and financial integration of the EU member states as well as the absence of any deeper economic shocks helped to hide these problems even further.

The need to develop risk-sharing mechanisms and implement reforms revealed serious differences between the EU countries. This resulted from the necessity to adopt new rights, obligations and a system of sanctions. Moreover, another problem for the integration stemmed from a tendency to solve the current issues at the intergovernmental level, i.e. beyond the EU institutions such as the European Commission or the European Parliament. Indeed, such solutions as the ESM or the Fiscal Compact are rather similar to intergovernmental agreements in their nature and may function with no connection to the EU as such.[30] Together with the Euro Plus Pact and the proposed banking union, these instruments clearly emphasised a division of countries into a two-speed Europe.

Evaluation of Proposed Reforms

Fiscal policy and fiscal union

According to theoretical assumptions, the best solution for the euro area is to establish a fiscal union with a common budget. In this case, the fiscal union

---

30 Barcz J., "Instrumenty międzyrządowe dotyczące kryzysu w strefie euro a spójność Unii. Możliwość przystąpienia państw członkowskich UE spoza strefy euro" (Cohesion of the European Union and Intergovernmental Instruments Regarding Euro Crisis. Possibility of Accession of Countries from beyond Eurozone), in: *Traktat z Lizbony. Wybrane zagadnienia*, Kenig-Witkowska M. M., Grzeszczak R. (eds.), Warszawa, 2012.

would provide ex-ante stabilisation instruments (and so fiscal risk-sharing) by means of transfers between countries, financial stability mechanisms and provision of public goods all for the union taken as a whole. It would also be necessary to set up a system of common taxes and give up much of national autonomy. The latter seems to be very unlikely in the short run, in light of all social and political considerations. This means that the future of the euro area's fiscal policy is going to be based upon the reformed SGP, the so-called Fiscal Compact and two-pack.[31]

In terms of fiscal policy, the proposed solutions seem to largely address the problems faced by the old SGP.[32] Firstly, in reaction to the SGP's weakness as regards inefficiency of the EU institutions in enforcing fiscal rules, a new mechanism was introduced providing more automatic fine imposition (Reversed Qualified Majority Voting (RQMV) in the EU Council. RQMV means that a recommendation or a proposal by the Commission is considered adopted in the Council unless a qualified majority of Member States votes against it. Whilst the RQMV is seen as the most important reform of the SGP, it fails to eliminate completely the risk of political actions and so still allows countries to evade sanctions. Secondly, significantly more attention was paid to ensuring the counter-cyclical nature of fiscal policy and its greater discipline in good times by the introduction of an expenditure rule. This may prevent such situations as those that occurred in Ireland and Spain, which, despite meeting the SGP rules, were affected by a serious breakdown of their public **finances when the bubble burst on the real estate market.** Unfortunately, before the crisis, both countries increased their structural

31 The Fiscal Compact (*Treaty on* Stability, Coordination and Governance in the Economic and Monetary Union) is an instrument intended to increase the efficacy of fiscal discipline among the euro area member states. It reiterates the fundamental SGP requirements to maintain fiscal stability and the maximum 3% deficit level or the 60% level of public debt in relation to GDP, and it also sets forth several additional elements. Most of all, it states that member states must introduce the so-called fiscal golden rule to their national legislation. This prohibits them to maintain structural deficit at a level above 0.5% of GDP. At the same time, sanctions for non-compliance can be imposed more automatically. Fines of up to 0.1% of GDP will be ordered by the EU Court of Justice, thus additionally depoliticising decisions.
Two-pack is a set of two regulations dedicated only for the euro area countries which aim is strengthening the surveillance mechanism in member countries.

32 Tchorek G., "Nierównowagi fiskalne i makroekonomiczne w strefie euro a nowe rozwiązania instytucjonalne" (Fiscal and Macroeconomic Imbalances in the Euro Area and New Institutional Regulations), Management and Business Administration. Central Europe, Akademia Leona Koźmińskiego, No. 2, 2013b.

spending, assuming that it was accompanied by structural revenues, which, in the end, turned out to be only cyclical. Thirdly, public debt was considered as a more important measure of fiscal policy quality because, as made evident by the crisis, it was the total debt rather than just deficit that might really determine a country's solvency (both the reformed SGP and the Fiscal Compact indicate the need to reduce total debt which exceeds 60% of GDP, or else sanctions must be imposed). Fourthly, a possibility was introduced to initiate the procedure of imposing sanctions upon countries for non-compliance with the SGP requirements already within its preventive arm. Fifthly, SGP is supplemented by the Council Directive specifying the so-called budgetary framework for member states which, among other things, provides for the establishment of fiscal councils by the end of 2013, the adoption of multi-annual financial planning and the independence of national statistical offices. Sixthly and perhaps most importantly, the reformed SGP, the two-pack and the Fiscal Compact constitute a two-stage mechanism of supervision over member states' fiscal policy at both Union and national levels.[33] Through effective implementation of these measures, the problem of the lack of ownership will be eliminated and national authorities will be more involved in coordination of fiscal and economic policies. This means that a number of obligations must be transferred to the national level. At the same time, the new instruments will enable the European institutions to monitor compliance in a more comprehensive way. They also comprise the European Semester, which is included in the six-pack and is also meant to form this kind of measure.[34]

The main threats to effectiveness of the new instruments include an increasing complexity of fiscal rules and prevailing broad discretion of the EU institutions, which may further hamper their enforcement.[35] Moreover, due to insufficient integration, the adopted solutions have not led to the development of a fiscal

---

33 Six-pack is a set of six regulation including reformed Stability and Growth Pact as well as new regulations related to Macroeconomic Imbalance Procedure (MIP).

34 The aim of the European Semester is to coordinate three following aspects of EU member states' economic policies: structural reforms defined under Europe 2020 Strategy, budgetary policy according to the revised SGP and macroeconomic policy as overseen under Macroeconomic Imbalance Procedure. The primary aim of this new coordination method is to introduce *ex-ante* procedures to replace the outgoing *ex-post* evaluation, which should allow for earlier detection of macroeconomic problems and implementation of appropriate solutions even before final budget-related decisions are made (Delors *et al*, 2012).

35 Schuknecht L., Moutot P., Rother P., Stark J., "The Stability and Growth Pact, Crisis and Reform", ECB Occasional Paper, 129, 2011, K. Marchewka-Bartkowiak, "Nowe ponadnarodowe reguły budżetowe odpowiedzią na kryzys zadłużenia publicznego

transfer mechanism initiated by the common budget in response to shocks (both symmetric and asymmetric). Even if the new solutions ensure fiscal discipline together with the so-called automatic stabilisers (within 3% budgetary deficit), episodes of serious turbulence (such as the recent financial crisis or by fiscal emergencies caused by other, for example climate-related, events) will require the initiation of substantial transfers exceeding the capacities of individual countries.[36] Accordingly, the necessity to accumulate a capital buffer against potential shocks will be a future challenge. Moreover, fiscal policy should constitute an instrument of counter-cyclical policy in the case of imbalances resulting from excessive allocation of resources in a specific segment of economic activity. While this is not a fundamental function of fiscal policy, it may complement the macro-prudential policy with adequate instruments for selective actions. Studies show that booms in real estate markets may be neutralised by, *inter alia*, tax impulses and the level of regulation in the real estate rental market (but also by instruments regulating access to financing – loan to value, debt to income.[37]

A further action should aim at establishing institutional legitimacy of fiscal councils in individual countries, as required under the six-pack and Fiscal Compact. This means that the effectiveness of solutions proposed will really depend on their implementation at the national level. What could be important in this context is coordination of work and exchange of experience among these institutions at the EU level, e.g. in the form of a European Fiscal Institute.[38] This corresponds to a cooperation model presented below, based upon relatively strong national institutions and European institutions equipped with mechanisms aimed at improving discipline.

Structural policy and competitiveness policy

The lack of structural and competitiveness policies has been one of the most serious weaknesses not only in the euro area but, in fact, in the entire European Union.

---

w strefie euro" (New Transnational Fiscal Rules – the Answer to Public Debt Crisis in the Euro Area), *Studia Ekonomiczne PAN*, 1, 2012.

36 Tchorek G., "Nierównowagi fiskalne i makroekonomiczne w strefie euro a nowe rozwiązania instytucjonalne" (Fiscal and Macroeconomic Imbalances in the Euro Area and New Institutional Regulations), Management and Business Administration. Central Europe, Akademia Leona Koźmińskiego, No. 2, 2013.

37 House Price Imbalances and Structural Features of Housing Markets, *Quarterly Report on the Euro Area*, European Commission, 2011.

38 M. Dunin-Wąsowicz, A. Darska, G. Tchorek, "Integracja europejska i nowy ład gospodarczy" (European Integration and the New Economic Order), *Scholar*, 2012.

The problems concerned both the EU (inefficiency of the Lisbon Strategy and the Open Method of Coordination) and the lack of policy stimulating national competitiveness. According to the laissez-faire doctrine of economic policy that prevailed in the 1990s, it was assumed that market-based mechanisms were going to replace structural and sectoral policies and that the changes triggered by adoption of the euro would contribute to higher competitiveness.

A procedure that is meant to provide an antidote to the above-mentioned problems is known as the Macroeconomic Imbalance Procedure (MIP). It involves an assessment of macroeconomic indices, which might potentially signal accumulation of imbalances.

The preventive dimension of the new procedure, which involves monitoring of the different economic areas, has been evaluated relatively well by economic experts.[39] Furthermore, the procedure establishes an economic pillar of the EMU that used to be seriously neglected because of the focus on fiscal policy. The instruments proposed under the procedure will probably make it possible to identify many of the sorts of problems that led to the crisis. Nonetheless, a weakness of the entire six-pack is the anti-crisis bias of the instruments, which do not provide solutions conducive to growth and increasing competitiveness. The procedure could better reflect a competition-stimulating environment and the Europe 202[40] priorities.[41] Another significant weakness of the adopted solutions is that they lack mechanisms for diminishing structural differences among countries, which would require the establishment of a common budget. Finally, the role of the macroprudential policy and of the European Systemic Risk Board (ESRB) recommendations, which should be followed by individual countries under the procedure seems to be insufficiently emphasised under MIP.[42] The experience of the crisis indicates that an uncontrolled integration of the euro area financial markets, in particular fast growth of credit, acted as a significant source of imbalances.[43]

---

39 Ch. Goodhart, *Europe: After Crisis*, DSF Policy Paper, 18, 2011.

40 Europe 2020 Strategy is a successor of Lisbon Strategy aiming to strengthen competitiveness of the EU economies.

41 Bastian J., Begg I., Fritz-Vannahme J., *Making the European Union work. Issues for Economic Governance Reform*, Synthesis of round-table discussions of the Expert Group on European, Economic Governance, Bertelsmann Stiftung, 3 March 2011.

42 European Systemic Risk Board and European Banking Authority (EBA) are the main institutions which were established after the crisis in order to strengthen financial regulatory and supervisory in the EU.

43 Giavazzi F., Spaventa L., "The European Commission's Proposals: Empty and Useless", www.voxeu.org, 2010.

What Kind of Integration Model for the EU and the Euro Area?

Barcz claims that the implemented institutional solutions mean that the main line of division among the EU member states will be that of whether they belong to the monetary union or not.[44] At the same time, he underlines that the new instruments also open up a possibility to differentiate between particular euro area countries. In case of breaking the rules, the European institutions will be able to punish individual euro area countries, which will be affected by a more restrictive system of sanctions than the rest of the EU member states.

As monetary integration proceeds, it will also be necessary to identify institutions responsible only for the euro area member states even if accessible to non-euro area countries. From the point of view of institutional efficiency, they should act as an effective instrument to mobilise members of the monetary union to conduct necessary structural reforms. Accordingly, deeper integration and broader competences of institutions responsible only for the euro area seem inevitable.[45]

It might mean that euro area membership may not be a crucial factor for countries' creditworthiness and political position. If we indeed expect positive outcomes of the new reforms and solutions, not only monetary integration should be taken into account. An important criterion for differentiating between particular EU countries should mainly stem from the quality of application of economic governance rules, and, to a lesser degree, from the stage of integration (these should certainly be interrelated). What is more, as established in six-pack and two-pack, the euro area member states can be punished with more severe sanctions than non-euro area countries. The main differences between countries could be based not only on new economic governance but also on implementation of the Single Market rules. This is in line with the identified causes of the present crisis, one of them being the countries' failure to ensure adequate conditions for integration of services sectors, which account for up to 70% of the euro area GDP.

Considering the limitations under which the European institutions are reformed, in particular the lack of prospects for deeper political integration,

---

44 Barcz J., "Instrumenty międzyrządowe dotyczące kryzysu w strefie euro a spójność Unii. Możliwość przystąpienia państw członkowskich UE spoza strefy euro" (Cohesion of the European Union and Intergovernmental Instruments Regarding Euro Crisis. Possibility of Accession of Countries from beyond Eurozone), w: *Traktat z Lizbony. Wybrane zagadnienia*, Kenig-Witkowska M. M., Grzeszczak R. (eds.), Warszawa, 2012.

45 If this fails to happen, the euro area and the EU will probably be exposed to next financial crises.

they should be structured upon the pattern of cooperation between the strong decision-making centre and relatively strong national institutions supported by well-designed and respected rules – according to the so-called hub and spoke delegation model[46] (see Figure 6.3).

Figure 6.3: Models of cooperation among the euro area institutions.

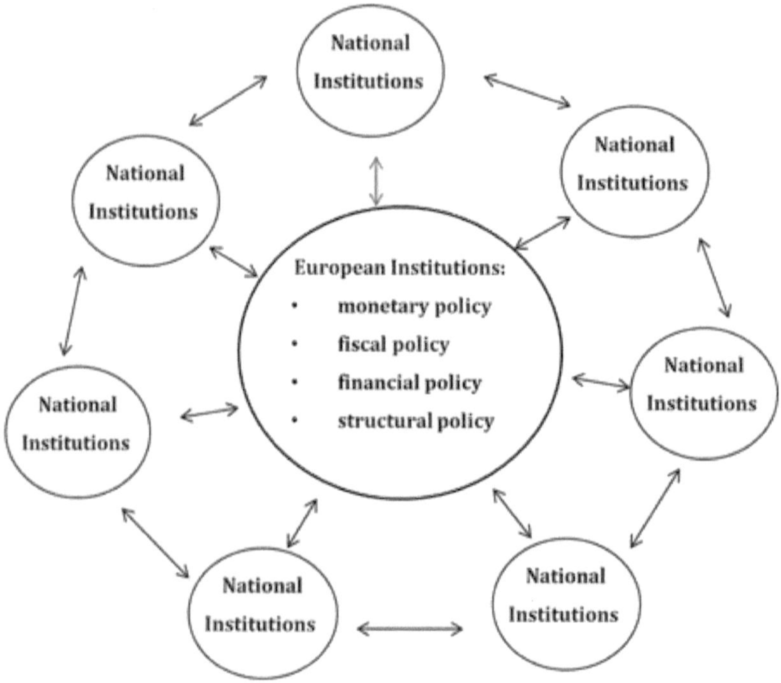

Source: Own summary.

46 In economic literature related to the economic geography, the hub and spoke model was used, among other things, to describe cooperation of firms and institutions in clusters. Goyal *et. al* proposed such a model as the optimum one from the point of view of the banking union in the euro area. Goyal R., Brooks P. K., Pradhan M., Tress T., DellAriccia D., Leckow R., *A Banking Union for the Euro Area*, IMF Discussion Staff Note, 2013.

Each European institution (responsible for monetary, fiscal, structural policies) should have a national counterpart, the latter one having the right, in cooperation with the decision-making centre, to adapt such common rules to local circumstances. This really holds true for almost all important areas of economic policy. One of the serious weaknesses of European integration has been weak transmission of rules between the central level and the local environment in which they are to be implemented. The above hub and spoke model requires consolidation of three following elements of the cooperation mechanism:

1. Decision-making centre – the euro area central institutions (with social and political legitimacy)
2. Broad and comprehensive legal and communication infrastructure (rules of cooperation).
3. National institutions (corresponding in their functions with the central level, having local social and political legitimacy).

This kind of structure may be seen as unrealistic due to the fact that a simple model as presented in Figure 6.4 does not reflect reality. Varying levels of political power of votes within institutions) and economic power (GDP level) of individual countries make it more probable for countries to form a kind of economic and political clubs. Factors favouring such a tendency may stem from common challenges or threats to a group of countries, which will not always be the same as the European interest. Moreover, the efficiency of the new institutional solutions will largely depend on the will to implement the relevant regulations at the national level (which often requires the establishment of new institutions) and the quality of this process.

In order for such a model to operate properly, it is important that the reformed and reinforced institutions cease to leave as much political and economical room for manoeuvre to member states as was the case prior to the crisis. This practice led to asymmetric maximisation of national interests and also created room for the *beggar thy neighbour policy*. The existing institutional system allowed for *asymmetry of power* (more political power enjoyed by larger than smaller countries), which led to *asymmetry of rationality*, enabling countries to prioritise national interests over the rationality (and indeed the efficiency) of the entire system.[47] The "strong central institutions – strong national institutions" model may be a better solution than the previous one (under which countries were in reality much

47 Grosse T.G., *Systemowe uwarunkowania kryzysu strefy euro* (*Systemic Determinants of the Euro Area Crisis*), Prawnicza i Ekonomiczna Biblioteka Cyfrowa, 2012.

stronger than the European institutions) and is frequently proposed as a model in which the European institutions clearly prevail over national ones. But full centralisation of governance with rigorous rules may constitute an element that makes the operation of the euro area ineffective in some areas. It seems that local authorities are sometimes better equipped to prevent pro-cyclicality of the centrally designed macro-economic policy. In the case of common monetary policy, it seems necessary to ensure decentralised (i.e. at national level) use of the remaining instruments, namely macro-prudential and fiscal policies. Such an institutional model is also in line with the EU's key principle, which is subsidiarity. National regulations can to some extent mitigate negative effects of *one size (does not) fit(s) all policy* and help avoid *boom and bust effects*, which were one of the main reasons for the euro area crisis.

No matter which model of cooperation is finally adopted, better efficiency of the euro area institutions will require some competence transfer to the central level. If the hub and spoke model is chosen, some serious risks may arise, including those stemming from potential conflicts between national and European institutions as well as from regulatory arbitrage which may occur due to differences in the way rules are shaped at the local level. The European Commission's role in safeguarding the rules of the Single Market should also increase. As a result, it seems necessary that there should be a transfer the pool of economic competences to the European level, mainly by the biggest member states. In view of extended powers of the decision-making centre as well as new local competences provided in order to avoid disputes and solve regulatory inconsistencies, it is important to give a mediatory role to one of the institutions in question (in a similar way as powers conferred to the EBA). Another important success factor will be the ability of the central authorities to rely on knowledge and competence of national bodies.

Joint Issuance of Bonds

In the short run, some EU and euro area member states face a number of serious interrelated problems resulting from the increase in public debt which has jumped abruptly since the crisis began, banking crisis and poor economic growth. To meet all of the above challenges, the EU needs financial resources which could be made available thanks through joint bond issuance.

On the one hand, this would help stimulate structural reforms and economic growth, and, on the other hand, cope with excessive debt, including the restructuring of some member states' debt. Moreover, debt *mutualisation* could also make it possible to use the opportunities of having the world's second international currency and well-developed financial markets. Joint bond issuance and a deeper fiscal risk-sharing process would require a deeper political union because jointly guaranteed debt securities would require countries involved to coordinate their fiscal policies in a better way.[48] Furthermore, the issuance of bonds would reduce the bankruptcy risk for the peripheral countries resulting from significant growth of their government bond yields.

The most important argument against joint issuance of bonds is a threat of weakening the incentives for fiscal discipline. The lack of market discipline to ensure the stability of public finance may be the main obstacle to joint issuance. In order to increase the credibility of joint bonds and eliminate moral hazard, it is necessary to have strong and reliable mechanisms ensuring fiscal, economic and financial discipline in the euro area countries. Another problem is the magnitude of debt accumulated during the crisis and its mutualisation.

Irrespective of the form of joint bonds, at an initial stage, they should only be issued on a minor scale by a central European institution and the ESM appears to be a natural candidate for this role. The benefits of the common euro area credibility should depend on satisfying of the criteria of financial and macro-economic stability under preventive and repressive parts of the EDP and MIP as well as on a country's commitment to comply with the macro-prudential policy rules.

Pillars of Monetary Integration

The foundation of the single currency on the power of institutions rather than on that of individual states should reduce the need for full political integration as its accompaniment, including the need to establish a common budget.[49] This, however, requires efficient operation of several unions: economic, fiscal and banking one, supported by the ESM and the ECB as the lender of last resort. As a condition of efficient operation of the model in question, an appropriate symmetry should be ensured between rights and obligations defined at both national and European levels. The following actions and elements seem necessary for the proper functioning of the euro area:

Firstly, high effectiveness of the economic governance rules concerning excessive macroeconomic imbalances and stability of public finance thanks to new solutions (six-pack, two-pack, European Semester, Fiscal Compact). On the one hand, an increased economic policy coordination, imposed by the MIP and

---

48 De la Dehesa G., *Eurobonds. Concepts and Implications*, Directorate General for Internal Policies, 2010.

49 According to historical plans, common budget should account for up to 25% of the monetary union GDP (Mcdoughal Report).

supported by a macro-prudential policy, used to monitor relations between the real and financial spheres, will reduce the systemic risk and the threat of crises. On the other hand, solutions in the field of fiscal policy should impose automatic economic stabilisers through accumulation of savings during good times and allowing for up to 3% of nominal deficit in rainy days.

Secondly, the establishment of a separate transfer budget for the euro area or an extension of financial potential of the existing EU budget. Wolff[50] (2012) indicates that the euro area's budget should account for ca. 2% of GDP of the entire monetary union and be available to the euro area countries and potentially also to the countries which intend to adopt the common currency and already are members of the ERM II (Exchange Rate Mechanism II) system.[51] Instead of a separate euro area budget, an increase in the EU budget with newly defined priorities for the competitiveness policy and a dedicated pool of funds earmarked for the euro area member states should be considered. As the common budget evolves towards greater strength and extended scope of structural activities, the social legitimacy of the EU's actions will be enhanced.

Thirdly, increasing financial capacity of the "European Monetary Fund," i.e. the ESM, with financial power equal to around 10% of the euro area's GDP. ESM could eventually constitute a financial backup for its role of LOLR *vis-à-vis* governments as well as two important pillars of the banking union: resolution mechanism and deposit guarantee system.

Fourthly, full banking union. The establishment of the banking union should make it possible to reduce risks in the banking sector through their early detection by means of the single supervisory mechanism. Moreover, the banking union with an adequate financial power ensured by the ESM should make it possible to eliminate the risk of contagion and fragmentation of financial markets.

Fifthly, it also seems desirable to create or improve the already existing national institutions whose competences correspond to those of the European institutions. In line with the subsidiarity principle, national authorities should, in justified cases and upon approval by the central institutions, have a possibility to correct, adjust and supplement the objectives and instruments created at the EU

---

50 Wolff G., *A Budget for Europe`s Monetary Union*, Bruegel Policy Contribution, No. 12, 2012.

51 Dullien and Torreblanca point out that a real influence on economic processes may be achieved with a budget of around 4–5% GDP. This, however, would entail the need to delegate the right to impose taxes to the European institutions. Dullien S., Torreblanca J.I., *What is political union?*, The European Council on Foreign Relation Policy Brief, 2012.

level. This requires better democratic legitimacy through consolidation of roles and competences of the central institutions (EC, EP) as well as national parliaments, also by authorisation of politically independent national institutions (fiscal councils, systemic risk boards).

Moreover, creation of additional impulses to increase financial market discipline should be considered, e.g. through changing the weights of investment risk attributed to government bonds, diversifying securities accepted by the ECB in refinancing operations depending on a country's rating or establishing exit rules from the euro area.

Finally, the issuance of common bonds should be an important way to achieve sufficient financial capacity and increase credibility. The role of common bonds and debt mutualisation should increase gradually and be accompanied by the enforcement of economic governance.

The solutions above should make it possible to accumulate financial resources amounting to 10–15% of the euro area's GDP. This capacity might stem from:

- automatic economic stabilisers (ca. 3% of GDP as regards admissible deficit at the level of individual countries),
- fiscal transfer thanks to the common budget (at 2% of EU GDP),
- full banking union and the ESM (10% of EU GDP).

This instrument should be accompanied by the possibility of taking advantage of the ECB's unlimited liquidity.

Most economists, politicians and societies seem to firmly believe in the deepening of integration but, at the same time, some resistance against the renunciation of more and more national autonomy is clearly visible. That is why the hub and spoke model really seems worth considering, with the following advantages taken into account:

- it may well be more effective than the present or highly centralised one,
- it is easier to implement because of evolutionary progress as regards the deepening of integration and can potentially eliminate many weaknesses experienced so far,
- it is more acceptable, both socially and politically, since it does not entail the necessity to create a large budget, accumulating several per cent of the euro area's GDP, which would probably require some form of political union to become reality.

Between the EU and the Euro Area

In many cases, solutions implemented in the EU increase the power of the decision-making centre, improve the infrastructure of communication between the centre and member states and also impose new obligations and sanctions on member states. One available way to be treated less rigorously under the existing procedures may be to remain outside the euro area because new regulations are more demanding for the monetary union member states. In such a way, the EU's new institutional model is going to deepen the present division into the euro area member states and other countries.

Two (or even several) speed Europe may entail some negative consequences for the countries that have not adopted the common currency. For example, the creation of a separate budget for the euro area may lower the importance and financial capacity of the EU budget, for its largest beneficiaries, including Poland. In a broader sense, being outside the monetary union will probably lower the political status of the non-euro area countries.

However, the political power of individual EU member states will not only result from the stage of institutional integration but will be based on their economic and financial power as well as their ability to build relations beyond the EU in the global environment.[52] The emergent institutional solutions also give the possibility to impose various sanctions on the euro area countries. Thus, the political status of a euro area country could also be diminished because of non-compliance with the common rules and obligations.

New EU member states (periphery) benefit from the fact that they operate very close to the euro area, which uses the second largest international currency in the world. Such a neighbourhood offers access to trade and investment ties as well as

52 It should be noted in this context that potential benefits of participation in the customs union between the EU and the USA will not depend on whether a country belongs to the euro area or remains outside the monetary union. Even if the customs union were only established for relations between the USA and the euro area, this would never preclude other countries not belonging to the euro area from benefitting from the union. Considering the geographic structure of political and business relations as well as the trade between the USA and the EU, the trade volume would most likely be increased through the United Kingdom, Ireland, Germany, France, Netherlands and Belgium.

new technology, a deep and liquid financial market, a reduced exchange rate risk thanks to a single exchange rate instead of eighteen different ones (one currency versus eighteen separate ones in the case of no monetary integration in Europe). Nonetheless, these countries may benefit from the euro area existence without official membership in the monetary union (like Denmark, Sweden, United Kingdom, and Lithuania, as well as other EU member states). While it is in a certain sense a form of *free ride,* it seems in many respects the best solution until real convergence is achieved at the level which minimises the risk related with abandoning a country's own monetary and exchange rate policy. Until such time, the euro area may play the role of economic, institutional and political anchor, while at the same time leaving the privilege of using national macro-economic policy instruments. Admittedly, what will prove crucial for sustainable growth of catching-up countries is their ability to run a counter-cyclical macroeconomic policy (fiscal, monetary, financial). The promotion of solutions ensuring compliance with the Single Market rules will be important for stability and integrity of the EU. In the particular case of Poland this requires the development of a strategy for presence in the EU as a country which heads toward the euro area at its own, rather than at an imposed, pace.[53]

Conclusions

The crisis in the euro area is a part of the global financial crisis. We have highlighted the fundamental economic and institutional assumptions of the euro area, which were made before the crisis, not only in the EU but, in fact, all over the global economic system. This means that the sources of the crisis in the euro area really extend beyond the mere inefficiency of the EU institutions. Nonetheless, there have been some evident mistakes made in the euro area establishment. Mainly due to political reasons and an optimistic approach, institutional solutions did not foresee any crisis management mechanisms.

The first part attempted to highlight mistaken macroeconomic assumptions behind the broad consensus in economic literature concerning monetary integration in the EU. As revealed, the crucial dysfunction of the euro area was the lack of mechanisms for:

---

53 In depth assessment of the Polish economy resilience during crisis as well as fulfilment of Maastricht criteria can be found in Polanski Z., *Poland During the Crisis: A "Green Island" Approaching the Euro Area?*, Holscher J. (ed.) *Poland and the Eurozone*, Studies in Economic Transition, Palgrave Macmillan, 2014.

- avoiding structural divergences and stimulating real convergence,
- financial market regulation,
- enforcing fiscal policy discipline and crisis management, including the LOLR role.

The latter part attempted to evaluate the institutional measures adopted aiming at increased efficiency in enforcing discipline in both fiscal and economic policy. These solutions may provide a significant step toward the reduction of systemic risk through the development of a two-stage control mechanism over fiscal and macroeconomic policy at both national and European level. However, they are characterised by anti-crisis bias, and thus fail to solve a serious problem of poor economic growth and the need to stimulate the EU member states' international competitiveness. Another issue is the necessity to control and reduce rapidly growing public debt. Measures that may be helpful in this respect include the issue of common bonds as an instrument of debt reduction and debt mutualisation as well as pro-growth measures. The establishment of the ESM as a permanent instrument, which may be used in case of crisis, is a very positive sign. However, its lending capacity needs to be extended. Another positive proposal is a greater role of the ECB in financial market stabilisation.

Despite more restrictive rules, the efficacy of the solutions adopted will depend on member states' will to implement and comply with them. It seems difficult, however, to make countries respect any common provisions unless they perceive the stability and competitiveness of the euro area and the EU as a matter of common interest. An efficient institutional system may not leave so much room for prioritising national interests over the EU interest. This suggests the need for a greater commitment to rules specified at the EU level, including an extension of the roles played by the European Commission, the European Parliament and national parliaments as well as independent national institutions as counterparts of the European institutions. This may be promoted by the suggested hub and spoke model, but it also requires giving up some of national autonomy, most of all by the EU's leading economies.

The new institutional system entails consequences for a further division into the euro area countries and countries unwilling to use the common currency. The reforms implemented will mostly regard countries bound by the common currency and only to a lesser extent other EU member states, not belonging to the euro area. Such a two-level arrangement, referred to as two-speed Europe, while having its weaknesses, ensures some flexibility of the system – something particularly desirable with respect to catching up countries. Membership in the EU alone makes it possible to benefit from integration and, largely, also from monetary integration, but staying outside the euro area gives more room for national policies until the countries complete real convergence process. However, a condition for such co-existence to be of any advantage is to have the entire European Union operation based upon the same foundations, laid down in the Single Market rules and accompanied by new economic governance rules. Staying outside the euro area should not exclude a country from the mainstream of integration because it is the economic and financial potential, and not only the institutional stage of integration, that really determines the status of a country. As the crisis has shown, economic power does not necessarily depend on whether a country uses the common currency or not.

Bibliography

Arghyrou M.G., Kontonikas A, (2011), *The EMU Sovereign-debt Crisis: Fundamentals, Expectation, and Contagion*, European Commission Economic Papers, No. 436.

Barcz J. (2012), *Instrumenty międzyrządowe dotyczące kryzysu w strefie euro a spójność Unii. Możliwość przystąpienia państw członkowskich UE spoza strefy euro*, in: *Traktat z Lizbony. Wybrane zagadnienia*, Kenig-Witkowska M. M., Grzeszczak R. (eds.), Warszawa.

Bastian J., Begg I., Fritz-Vannahme J. (2011), *Making the European Union Work. Issues for Economic Governance Reform*, Synthesis of round-table discussions of the Expert Group on European, Economic Governance, Bertelsmann Stiftung, 3.

Bijlsma M., Valee S. (2012), *The Creation of the Euro Area Financial Safety Nets*, Bruegel Working Paper 2012/09, 2012.

Blanchard O., Giavazzi F. (2002), *Current Account Deficits in the Euro Area. The End of the Feldstein Horioka Puzzle?*, NBER Working Papers 8120, National Bureau of Economic Research.

Bobeva D., (2013), "The New EU Macroeconomic Imbalances Procedure and its Relevance for the Candidate Countries", *Journal of Central Banking Theory and Practice.*

De la Dehesa G. (2010), *Eurobonds, Concepts and Implications*, Directorate General for Internal Policies.

De Santis S. (2012), *The Euro Area Sovereing Crisis. Save Haven, Credit Ratings Agencies and the Spread of the Fever from Greece, Ireland and Portugal*, ECB Working Paper No. 1419.

Delors J., S. Fernandes, E. Mermet (2011), *The European Semester: Only a First Step*, Notre Europe, Policy Brief, No. 22.

Delpla J., Von Weizsäcker J. (2011), *Eurobonds: The Blue Bond Concept and Its Implications*, Bruegel Policy Contribution, 2011/02.

Dinga M., Dingova V. (2011), *Currency Union and Investment Flows: Estimating the Euro Effect on FDI*, IES Working Paper: 25/2011.

Dullien S., Torreblanca J. I. (2012), *What is Political Union?*, The European Council on Foreign Relation Policy Brief.

Dunin-Wąsowicz M., Darska A., Tchorek G. (2012), "Integracja europejska i nowy ład gospodarczy", *Scholar*.

Duval R., Elmeskov, J. (2006), *The Effects of EMU on Structural Reforms in Labour and Product Markets*, ECB Working Paper No. 596.

Eichengreen B., Hausmann R., Panizza U. (2003), *Currency Mismatches, Debt Intolerance and Original Sin: Why They Are Not the Same and Why it Matters*, NBER Working Paper No. 10036.

Elliott D.J. (2012), *Key Issues on European Banking Union*, Global Economy & Development Working Paper No. 52, Brookings.

European Commission (2011), *House Price Imbalances and Structural Features of Housing Markets*, Quarterly Report on the Euro Area, http://ec.europa.eu/economy_finance/publications/qr_euro_area/2011/pdf/qrea3_section_4_en.pdf.

Filipek A.,K., Schreiber T. (2010), *The Stability and Growth Pact: Past Performance and Future Reforms*, Working Papers 97, Department of Economics, College of William and Mary Foreign Relations (ECFR).

Flam H., Nordström H. (2007), *Euro Effects on the Intensive and Extensive Margins of Trade*, IIES.

Frankel, J.A., Rose, A.K. (1998), *The Endogeneity of the Optimum Currency Area Criteria*, NBER Working Papers, 5700, National Bureau of Economic Research,

Gianviti F., Krueger A.O. Pisani-Fery J, Sapir A., von Hagen J. (2010), *A European mechanism for sovereign debt crisis resolution: a proposal*, Bruegel.

Gianviti F., Krueger, A.O. Pisani-Fery, J., Sapir, A. von Hagen, J. (2010), *A European Mechanism for Sovereign Debt Crisis Resolution: APproposal*. Bruegel Blueprint Series, 10.

Giavazzi, F., Spaventa, L. (2010), *The European Commission's Proposals: Empty and Useless*, http://www.voxeu.org/article/european-commission-s-proposals-empty-and-useless.

Goodhart Ch. (2011), *Europe: After Crisis*, DSF Policy Paper, 18.

Goyal R., Brooks P.K., Pradhan M., Tress T., DellAriccia G., Leckow R. (2013), *A Banking Union for the Euro Area*, IMF Discussion Staff Note.

Goyal R., Brooks P.K., Pradhan M., Tressel T., DellAriccia G., Leckow R. (2013), *A Banking Union for the Euro Area*, IMF Discussion Staff Note.

Gros D. (2012), *Macroeconomic Imbalances in the Euro Area: Symptom or Cause of the Crisis?*, CEPS Policy Brief, 266, Centre for European Policy Studies.

Gros D., Mayer T. (2012), *Liquidity in Times of Crisis: Even the ESM Needs It*, CEPS Policy Brief, No. 265.

Grosse T.G. (2012), *Systemowe uwarunkowania kryzysu strefy euro*, Prawnicza i Ekonomiczna Biblioteka Cyfrowa.

Hallerberg M., Marzinotto B., Wolff, G.B. (2012), *On the Effectiveness and Legitimacy of EU Economic Policies*, Bruegel Policy Paper, 4.

Hauptmeier S., Sanchez-Fuentes J., Schuknecht L. (2011), "Towards Expenditure Rules and Fiscal Sanity in the Euro Area", *Journal of Policy Modeling*, 33.

IMF (2009), *Lessons of the Global Crisis for Macroeconomic Policy*, https://www.imf.org/external/np/pp/eng/2009/021909.pdf.

Kalemi–Ozkan S., Sorensen B.E., Yosha O. (2001), "Regional Integration, Industrial Specialization and the Asymmetry of Shocks across Regions", *Journal of International Economics.*

Kinoshita Y. (2011), *Sectoral Composition of Foreign Direct Investment and External Vulnerability in Eastern Europe*, IMF, Working Paper.

Larch M., van den Noord P., Joung L. (2010), *The Stability and Growth Pact: Lessons from the Great Recession*, European Economy. Economic Paper, No.429.

Laski K., Podkaminer, L. (2012), *The Basic Paradigms of EU Economic Policy-Making Need to Be Managed.* Cambridge Journal of Economics, 36(1).

Lehwald S. (2012), *Has the Euro Changed Business Cycle Synchronization? Evidence from the Core and the Periphery*, Ifo Working Paper No. 122.

Marchewka-Bartkowiak, K. (2012), "Nowe ponadnarodowe reguły budżetowe odpowiedzią na kryzys zadłużenia publicznego w strefie euro", *Studia Ekonomiczne PAN*, No.1.

Merler, S., Pisani-Ferry, J. (2012), *Sudden Stops in the Euro Area*, Bruegel Policy Contribution, 12.

Miles W. and VIJVERBERG C. (2011), *The Exogeneity (at Best) of the Optimum Currency Area Criteria for the Euro Zone* Wichita State University working paper available at https://www.gc.cuny.edu/.../The-Exogeneity-CUNY-2.

Mitra P. (2011), *Capital Flows to EU New Member States: Does Sector Destination Matter?* IMF, WP.

Mongelli F. (2002), *New Views on the Optimum Currency Area Theory: What is EMU Telling Us?*, ECB Working Paper No. 138.

Mongelli F. P., De Grauwe P. (2005), *Endogeneities of Optimum Currency Areas: What Brings Countries Sharing a Single Currency Closer Together?*, ECB Working Paper No. 468.

Mroczek W. (2009), "Wpływ wprowadzenia euro na stopień otwartości i zmiany strukturalne w handlu krajów strefy euro", in: *Raport na temat pełnego uczestnictwa Rzeczypospolitej Polskiej w trzecim etapie Unii Gospodarczej i Walutowej.*

Oręziak L. (2004), *Finanse Unii Europejskiej*, Warsaw: PWN.

Petroulas P. (2007), "The Effect of the Euro on Foreign Direct Investment", *European Economic Review*, 51.

Pisani-Ferry J., Wolff G.B. (2012), *Fiscal Implication of a Banking Union*, Bruegel Policy Brief, No. 2/2012.

Rogowski W. (2013), *Unia bankowa - notatki z placu budowy*, in: *Wyzwania regulacji rynków finansowych*, Rogowski W. (ed.), Oficyna Allerhanda.

Polanski Z. (2014), *Poland During the Crisis: A "Green Island" Approaching the Euro Area?*, Holscher J. (ed.), *Poland and the Eurozone*, Studies in Economic Transition, Palgrave Macmillan.

Schuknecht L., Moutot, P., Rother, P., Stark, J. (2011), *The Stability and Growth Pact, Crisis and Reform*, ECB Occasional Paper, 129.

Sinn H. W., Buchen T., Wollmershäuser T. (2011), *Trade Imbalances - Causes, Consequences and Policy Measures*: Ifo's Statement for the Camdessus Commission. CESifo Forum.

Sławiński A. (2012), "Strefa euro: Scenariusz alternatywny", *Fola Oeconomica*, No. 273, Uniwersytet Łódzki.

Sousa J., Lochard J. (2011), "Does the Single Currency Affect FDI?", *The Scandinavian Journal of Economics*, Volume 113, Issue 3.

Tchorek G. (2013), *Czy można odnosić korzyści z integracji walutowej?*, w: *Mechanizmy funkcjonowania strefy euro*, Owsiak S. (ed.), Cracow: Wyd. Krakowska Szkoła Biznesu Uniwersytetu Ekonomicznego w Krakowie.

Tchorek G. (2013), *Nierównowagi fiskalne i makroekonomiczne w strefie euro a nowe rozwiązania instytucjonalne*, Management and Business Administration. Central Europe, Akademia Leona Koźmińskiego, No 2.

Tchorek G. (2014), "Źródła kryzysu a nowe rozwiązania instytucjonalne w strefie euro", *Finanse* (7).

Vernengo M., Perez-Caldentey E. (2012), *The Euro Imbalances and Financial Deregulation: A Post-Keynesian Interpretation of the European Debt Crisis*, Working Paper No. 702, Levy Economics Institute.

Wolff G. (2012), *A Budget for Europe's Monetary Union*, Bruegel Policy Contribution, No. 12.

Zaleska M. (ed.) (2013), *Unia bankowa*, Difin.

Alojzy Z. Nowak, Kazimierz Ryć,
Yochanan Shachmurove

Economic Policy After the Financial Crisis

Introduction

As the present crisis continues, it is hard to see when the turbulence in the global economy is going to cease. Still, a question arises: since economies emerge from the recent crisis, what are the lessons economists and policy makers should take away and draw for economic policy? In both economic and political literature, the heated debates unfold about the crisis – its sources, consequences, and methods of recovery.

Policy makers are now more knowledgeable about the nature of the crisis, its reasons, and its effects. Due to the strong remedies applied by governments and central banks, the gross domestic product (GDP) did not fall as dramatically in the recent crisis as it did during the crisis of the late 1920s and early 1930s. Yet, other serious consequences, such as high unemployment, could adversely affect productivity, and cause economic unrest and stagnation. The social consequences of the crisis are also high on the list of issues for debate. This article deals with the social aspects of economic policy: specifically, the social effects of a neo-liberal model of economic policy. Furthermore, it discusses the issues of unemployment and national income distribution.

Two Stages of Development Prior to the Crisis

After World War II, capitalism experienced two stages of relatively peaceful growth. Well-developed countries of Western Europe and North America, mainly those associated in the Organisation of Economic Co-operation and Development (OECD), enjoyed almost thirty years of dynamic and sustainable development.

During that period, these countries had high and rising GDP per head, low unemployment, low inflation, and significant attenuation of business cycles. The standard of living in Western societies increased, accompanied by a growth in real wages. The gap between the pay of regular workers and that of management remained at a reasonably low level. The social safety of all workers, including the secured employees and those with social security benefits, was consolidating. Wage and salary earners started to become involved with the management and shareholding of a company. At that stage of development, capitalism – as it had developed in Europe – received such names as: welfare state, social market economy, and Rhineland model of capitalism (see Albert, 1993, Albert and Gonenc, 1996, Hall and Soskice, 2001).

This type of capitalistic system development broke down in the mid-1970s. Its demise was a result of externalities and hardships experienced by the American economy, as it attempted to combine building a great society with a costly war and an arms race. This resulted in the elimination of the US Dollar gold standard and the demise of the Bretton Woods accords, which, in turn, caused much tension, turbulence, and uncertainty in financial markets.

Wars and tensions in the Middle East, together with the weakening of the US Dollar, stimulated the activity of the international oil cartel known as the Organization of the Petroleum Exporting Countries (OPEC). This caused oil prices to rise, turbulence in monetary markets, high inflation, and a high rate of unemployment. The combination of simultaneous inflation and unemployment, i.e. stagflation, no longer fitted the assumptions of the Keynesian doctrine, which had prevailed during that epoch of capitalism. It was necessary to revise the doctrine of economic policy based on J.M. Keynes' theory. The situation was aggravated by the difficulty in implementing the welfare state and ineffectiveness of policy due to excessive bureaucracy, extravagant public spending, high public debt, and impaired motivation to work.

Keynesian economics gave way to ultraliberal neoclassical doctrine, modelled upon a policy called Thatcherism in the United Kingdom and Reaganomics in the United States. This policy emphasised free operation of market-based mechanisms, deregulation, small government, frugal budgets, low taxes, and a liberalised unregulated labour market. Over time, the doctrine also known as the "Washington Consensus," (see also Chapter 1 of this work) was recommended to all countries, especially to those applying for aid from the International Monetary Fund (IMF) and the World Bank (Williamson, 1989).

The new policy provided an impulse for growth. It helped to control inflation and maintained the rate of economic growth, while not quite achieving the level of the previous stage. The latter stages of this new era of ultraliberalism witnessed a wholesale deregulation of the financial sector including the liberalisation of international capital flows and this together with worldwide globalisation in general spurred development and caused rapid increases in GDP in developing countries. OECD countries could access foreign markets, exploit their much cheaper productive resources and gain opportunities capital expansion. However, over time, the tension and imbalances increased due to the carrying over of manufacturing processes by industrial corporations of well-developed countries to low-wage countries. The present crisis may (at least to some extent) emerge from these negative effects.

While the associated reallocation of resources improved efficiency of both corporations and the global economy as a whole, it also altered the global labour distribution. In particular, it brought deindustrialisation to the West and economic development to the countries in the East.

The 2008 crisis took both economists and politicians by surprise. Since the very beginning, a voluminous literature has focussed on the crisis and what caused it:

1. First, the emergence of a dramatic growth of the income gap between the middle class and the top 1% of countries' financial earners. American CEOs used to earn 20 times as much as its company's average employee. Today, in the US, a CEO in the top 100 corporations earns 320 times more (Buras 2012). Other leading capitalistic countries show similar patterns. Until recently, the growth of the difference in the standard of living between the upper and middle class is small. In fact, the elites appropriated the effects of the domestic product growth.
2. The financialisation of the global economy, financial institutions, markets, etc., continue to increase in size and influence at the expense of the sectors of real economy: industry, agriculture, trade and others. For instance, the stock market is performing well, not because the price of commodities is increasing, but because its financing depends on certain individuals with increasing incomes. Independent existence of financial processes (i.e. financial operations) made with remote links to the real economy was facilitated by increasing supplies of liquid loanable funds coming from the ever increasing income of corporate and individual financial elites. A financial game dubbed as "casino capitalism" (Strange 1986) is played out with little regard to the shrinking of investments in the real sphere.
3. The transfer of jobs from well-developed countries to the countries considered as emerging markets. In effect, this undermines the bargaining position of workers in wealthy countries and restricts the growth of real wages. Unprecedented access to credit markets alleviated stagnation of real income of workers in advanced countries and enabled consumption growth financed by debt. In the United States, for many families, mortgage debt became the way to finance additional consumption. Homes and real estate purchased on credit and mortgaged were used as collateral for further credits as long as their prices were increasing. Homeowners used their house, purchased on credit, as a kind of cash machine to pay for cars or expensive renovations. As a consequence, a large portion of toxic assets started to appear in banks' portfolios.

4. The low interest rates and an excess supply of loanable funds, resulting from high level of savings among the Chinese, which increased from 38% up to 54% of the country's GDP in the years 2000–2006 alone, financed the acquisition of the US government bonds, raising their prices and lowering their rate of return. Savings skimmed from Asia topped up the funds emanating from oil-exporting countries, invested in sovereign investment funds. The overall abundance of capital resulted in low interest rates and high accessibility to credit markets. These aggregated factors created conditions for excessive indebtedness of households and enterprises in many countries. This was particularly evident in the housing and real estate sectors as well as other durable goods markets. They also encouraged the authorities in a number of countries to cover the public sector spending with credit, as the costs of debt servicing were so low.
5. Decreased risk of inflation. The transfer of industrial production from wealthy countries to countries with cheap labour resulted in reduced costs and prices of commodities involved in international trade exchange, i.e. globally traded goods. The same holds with respect to services provided digitally. A decrease of the price index for traded goods and services prevented a growth in inflation rates in developed countries. The situation favoured expansionary monetary regimes and expansive budgetary policies applied in many countries.
6. The lack of regulation or control by governments and central banks over creation and application of new financial instruments. This mainly relates to the instruments used to dilute the risk and hinder its appraisal. Emerging toxic assets undermined the reliability of financial institutions, drove many reputable banks and insurers to bankruptcy or at the very edge of it, and eventually led them to freeze cash flow and credit. The OECD countries allocated hundreds billions of dollars to save banks from bankruptcy. The sums spent by the governments of Western European countries to bail out the banks that had acquired the toxic US assets increased their public debt. According to various estimations, the remedies caused their public debt to rise from an average of 60% up to 80% of GDP (*Rzeczpospolita*, 2012).

The Crisis of Public Finance

The crisis stemming from private debt changed into public debt as banks were bailed out with public money. Moreover, a decline in production caused by the transfer of the banking crisis onto the real sphere of the economy (through a credit crunch and confidence effects on investment) resulted in a reduction of tax revenues while government expenditures were increasing. A growth of budget deficits and of public debt increased uncertainty in financial markets. What followed was a drop in demand for government bonds, reducing prices of bonds and increasing debt service costs (interest on public debt). This implied either a crisis of public finance or a serious threat of such a crisis in many countries, adding up to a rather uncomfortable condition for neoliberal economists and politicians subscribing to their ideas.

Market-based mechanisms failed, the market was blamed, and the State was stigmatised. This caused many publicists and economists to blame excessive public spending. However, the truly welfare states, such as the Nordic countries, have not experienced financial crises. Instead, this kind of hardship affects governments that are excessively "friendly," or accommodating to their citizens, eager to bear high public costs combined with low taxes. Greece, perhaps, is the best example of such a "friendly" state; although it is hard to observe many welfare features or extensive social benefits, it still managed to accumulate vast public debt. Low interest rates encourage people to borrow and the government to fund social benefits, build extensive administrative structures which create more government jobs, while at the same time taxpayers are treated with a "soft hand." Government bonds, used to pay for such expenses, are likely to find their way directly or indirectly to the portfolios of the wealthier segments of society. Bonds are typically seen as a good low-risk liquid investment,. This way everybody supposedly wins, the poor and the rich alike.

Let us, then, leave aside the problem of identifying the causes of public debt. If it has become excessive in a number of countries, it was not only due to its volume but also due to markets being ill disposed to fund it. It becomes more and more difficult to sell subsequent tranches of government bonds issued. It is particularly telling to support the point that this has more to do with market appraisal, than it has to do with the size of public debt the Japanese example. The country has enormous public debt, in excess of twice its GDP. However, Japan still has no problem with its cheap funding and servicing. The reason is that the debt is largely denominated in the domestic currency and as such, it is less exposed to speculative capital. An excessive indebtedness of governments requires private saving to increase. The more a large and increasing public debt is seen as a liability by financial markets, i.e. involving higher risk for investors, the higher the private savings needed, and this is painful for the voters.

Furthermore, when countries that are trade partners both implement policy to increase savings, this tends to reduce domestic demand and therefore impair country's imports. The negative GDP growth, caused by shrinking domestic and external demand, decreases tax revenues which only increases already high government deficits. The consequence of this vicious cycle often increases rather than reduces debt.

This may create a strong desire to deploy measures to control the debt increase. The goal is to convince markets of the positive prospects for ultimate escape from the vicious cycle of ever-mounting debt and to encourage international investment funds to acquire debt instruments at a price reasonably attractive to the issuer. The result is that the opinion of international financial markets and even manipulators becomes more important than the state's development objectives or aspiration of its citizens.

The policy of increasing private saving and restraining budgetary deficits applied in parallel tends to result in reduced growth rate and in countries, keen on radical restriction of pubic outlays, as is the case in Greece, Italy or Spain, leads to recession. In reality, these countries should expect their economy to suffer from stagnation for several years. Expansionary monetary policy cannot reignite staggering economies as the demand for credit by both households and corporations shrinks anyway. Households reckon with the uncertainty of employment and income, and often also with debt overhangs from past spending splurges, while enterprises postpone crucial investments due to low demand and low prospects. As a result, the attempts to bring about economic growth and an increase employment fail.

Market-Based Mechanisms and the Need to Reduce Unemployment

Because economic policy since 2008 has proved unable to ensure relatively full employment, it is improper to insist endlessly on applying the principles of neoliberal economics and maintaining the rules of the Washington Consensus. Those policies of restrictive monetary policy, small government, low tax rates, flexible labour legislation, deregulation, privatisation, and free markets, have signally failed to work in many economies. NO best single solution exists for any economy. Neoliberal economists, adherent to the current school of thought in macro-economy that has prevailed until quite recently, keep on repeating their mantra: "in order to stimulate the economy, taxes should be lowered and employment has to become more flexible."

Moreover, they have maintained this belief in the prosperous period prior to the crisis, during the crisis, and in the recovery period after the crisis. They still expect and demand the same results from the same toolbox. This is not just adherent loyalty to the rules of the Washington Consensus – actually, it deepens the problem. Consequently, this implies even more junk contracts (without a real job contract) for workers, lower labour costs and lower minimum wages, as wages represent costs. In the case of regular employees, wages are nothing but cost and – like all kinds of costs – must be minimised, even when profit margins grow and financial accumulation is funnelled to liquid assets rather than allocated for real investments.

In effect, all bonuses not spent on consumption are undistributed profits of corporations and contribute to decreasing domestic demand. The growth of a pool of liquid assets fosters the process of financialisation of the economy, further tearing the sphere of finance apart from the real sphere.

While highlighting the need to undertake actions reaching beyond the rules resulting from the Washington Consensus, we are not proposing any wholesale renunciation of the rules of free market economy. Historical experience teaches that the actions of the "invisible hand" are still the best way to meet the needs of societies. Prices shaped by the free market reflect the value of a given commodity or service and the cost of such commodity or service for its manufacturer/provider, including the society. As we follow the market price, we consider both benefits and costs of what we do. To quote a popular handbook:

> *...a price influences decisions of individual, enterprises, and households so that they behave in the way which, in many cases, implies maximization of profit for the society as a whole.* (Mankiw, Taylor 2009:40)

What seems fitting here is to emphasise the words "in many cases." The market-based mechanism shapes the level of GDP, and therefore society's welfare, to the extent to which it depends upon *per capita* product. According to this logic, where one interferes with the action of the market-based mechanism (for example, through raising tax burdens) this negatively affects the allocation of assets. By disturbing the natural mechanism for reaching an equilibrium price, one undermines, partly at least, the effects of the invisible hand. The same principle applies, even to a higher degree, when one is tempted to regulate prices, e.g. of food or rents. In fact, we have to deal with a certain inconsistency in the assumption. The invisible hand may only be effective where the state operates in the "right way." By that, we mean when the state collects taxes for providing legislation, enforcing its application, and ensuring safety. These are all essential for any market to operate. At the very beginning of free market doctrine, we find the need to separate the maximum of product enabled by market valuation of goods and market allocation from social welfare. This includes not only the value of products but also such issues as safety and public order and organisation achieved at the cost of taxes.

Furthermore, one needs to consider the following factors:

- Imperfection of market allocation of assets, in particular in the area of material and social infrastructure (health, science, education);
- Side effects of actions, which negatively affect welfare of others (externalities);
- Negative consequences of monopoly advantages for evaluation of resources and for other people's welfare.

Welfare is not identical with the level of *per capita* GDP, although it partly depends on the level of *per capita* GDP. The above-mentioned market imperfections confirm this point, if only indirectly. In this context, other circumstances also increase the gap between the level of GDP and welfare or quality of life.

First, it is the meeting of fundamental material needs at an adequately high level – considering that the needs mass consumers have are such as the producer develops for them and tells them to have. Such a practice is not bad as such, because it usually improves the living standard of consumers. However, it also increases a number of abuses stemming from an advantage producers have over consumers. This deepens the difference between the level of *per capita* product and welfare of the society, contributing at the same time to excessive consumption of non-renewable resources.

Second, this market-based mechanism may generate and deepen social inequalities leading to profound income stratification. The problem has been debated for quite a while now and gives rise to a great deal of controversy. Some tend to put forth the opposition between efficiency and social egalitarianism; others argue about the need to conceive efficiency of the social system in a more comprehensive way so that the inequality of opportunities is cumulatively increased by the inequality of income with negative effects to development, also in terms of economic growth. Unemployment is also an example of market inefficiency, although neoliberal economists tend to blame either the actions of the State or trade unions.

Under the conditions of a free market, economic growth does not necessarily reduce the unemployment – in fact, it may seriously increase it. This is not only because technology has improved, thereby displacing some labour, but it is also because of other factors. Jeremy Rifkin (2003), who argued that rising unemployment is the result of a rapid rise in labour productivity, publicised this phenomenon some years ago. Other factors relevant in this context include the already mentioned deindustrialisation of developed countries, with production being transferred to emerging markets as well as ill adaptation of labour resources in Western countries to the new types of work in highly advanced sectors.

Unemployed people do not generate domestic product. Many people who have temporarily lost their jobs because of labour market hysteria remain, in fact, jobless on a permanent basis. Whereas unneeded machinery is scrapped, an unemployed labour force should be re-employed by using non-market mechanisms to improve the level of welfare, where the market proves unable to generate the requisite demand for labour.

The Necessity to Restore Sector-Specific Policy

In order to achieve a condition close to full employment, a state economic policy should focus upon job-generating sectors even if the impact on the market appears negative, i.e. where revenues fail to cover the costs or even where revenues are not there at all. But, still the employed contribute to the growth of welfare, which is intangible in market terms.

It is probably too late to restore a real industrial policy and to create jobs by supporting industrial development using protectionism. Protectionism may work in the short run. However, in the long run it decreases competition and innovation. Consequently, it creates trade wars, lay-offs, and costumer dissatisfaction. This is prevented today now by the high degree of national economy integration with the global economy, membership in the World Trade Organization (WTO) and in the European Union or other regional blocs such as MERCOSUR or ASEAN as well as by mutual obligations resulting from other international agreements.

In these circumstances, it is necessary to return to non-commercial sectors by putting them to good use – including education, health, science, and culture. Also important in this context are family-supportive policies and development of a small child-care sector.

Sector-based policy is a solid and well-rooted element of advanced market economies. Agricultural policy, properly appreciated in most countries, is a good example. Dynamic growth of the second sector, i.e. industry and construction, allowed countries to leave inefficient agriculture aside, which was manifested to perhaps the highest extent in Japan during the stage of the most dynamic growth when a strong export sector was developed and vast areas of inefficiency were left in agriculture and services.

At present, we are witnessing the notorious problem of a domestic trade sector in India. Opening of trade to megastores, planned by the government, is seen as a threat to small-scale commerce, which provides jobs to 220m citizens, hence the strong protest in its defence.

Non-commercial sectors of the economy must not be regarded as relics of traditional economy. As it was mentioned above, they are areas to look for additional employment in order to alleviate labour market tensions resulting from unemployment. In fact, they may potentially become a durable – or even leading – element of the economy.

Over time, voluminous literature has arisen dedicated to the importance of education, science, health care, and sound demographic proportions fostering social and economic growth in the long run. However, the present efforts being made at saving in the public sector, resulting from the crisis of public finance, divert government activities in an opposite direction, namely – to the budget cuts. This also relates to the portion allocated to health, education, science, and culture, thus contributing to further aggravation of the unemployment problem. It is very rarely (for reasons of political expediency, especially in representative democracies) that governments raise taxes in order to balance their budgets, especially with regard to income taxes. Nevertheless, it is both possible and desirable to change the present policy, although this change is not easy or prompt. What may prove decisive here are political factors: it is actually necessary to take off the golden straitjacket.

The "golden straitjacket" is the term Thomas Friedman used to describe a strategy applied by governments, which insist on restrictive application of the Washington Consensus, i.e. healthy currency, low taxes, flexible labour legislation, and private free trade. The goal is to earn market trust, attract capital, and to improve one's reputation with investment funds and ratings agencies (see Rodrik 2011). The straitjacket is meant to restrict government's economic policy. The loyalty to those principles as well as good reviews and trust from the markets acts as a political recommendation to governments.

The opposition, where it comes to power, is not going to give up these rules either. Accordingly, the policy in question is consistent with the expectations and demands of financial markets and of a country's financial elites, while not necessarily so – as mentioned above – with aspirations or objectives of society as a whole. Governments have arguments, or rather an alibi, strong enough to carry on with such policy.

Sector-specific policy emphasises development of non-commercial public services, funded by the State budget and, in particular, using funds from tax revenues rather than the method of "friendly" State. This means taking that protective straightjacket off. There are, in our opinion, significant arguments advocating a departure from that one-sided and opportunistic policy for the sake of one which fosters the development of the public services sector. The arguments are as follows:

1. There is no evidence to support the claim that lower income taxes, in particular, lower tax progression translate into increased employment. Similarly, there is no evidence that higher income taxes and steeper tax progression restricts entrepreneurship and innovation. Statistical research of such relationships yields ambiguous outcomes.

2. This means that in the case of the public finance crisis, cutting spending on public services, with the consequence of decreased domestic demand and deepened recession, is not the best way to handle the situation. In these conditions, it is better to increase tax revenues, especially through income tax. This certainly does not suggest that justification of public services expenditure is not required, or neglected.
3. Expenditures for development and proper quality of nursery schools, kindergartens and schools to help working mothers and multi-children families are a better investment than investing the resources of pension funds in the stock market. A large number of healthy and well-educated future workers provide a security for future pensions. Just as in the case of pro-natal policy, there are a number of arguments to advocate efforts for development and quality improvements in public education. Raising the quality of public schools is a pre-condition needed to equalise opportunities for the youth. Schools of any level are the most important element for future development. Of course, the increased spending allocated to that end needs support from a well-prepared organisation and management. Today that may also imply in the secondary schools of many advanced countries a need for not only a tough and rigorously inspected academic curriculum but also for a clear policy concerning student discipline and its enforcement. This is particularly important in the inner city schools of many of the worlds' metropolises.
4. The outlays for health care and for the elderly have increased significantly in all countries, including those applying neo-liberal principles in their economic policies. Across developed countries, we find increasing average lifetimes as well as highly developed medical technologies. While there may in certain countries be room for efficiency improvements in healthcare it is politically inevitable that these increasing costs will continue to need to be funded. The health protection system, including care for the ill and disabled, provides an extremely broad area for a socially justified growth of employment (see Baumol, Tobin 1989:1160–1162).
5. Another extensive area for professional activity emerges from the animation of culture, recreation, and sports. More substantial, public funds allocated to these fields, if spent reasonably and properly, may bring similarly beneficial effects as those dedicated to education, science and health care in the long-term, increasing human and social capital.

Outlays on services and benefits funded by public resources contribute to welfare and society's standard of living – factors not specifically reflected in the domestic product indexes. To be sure, in the long run, they contribute to a growth of a GDP.

Unfortunately, tangible effects in economic terms will not occur immediately, since expenses have to be borne now. Nonetheless, it is necessary – both to improve people's welfare and to avoid social unrest arising from long-lasting unemployment, especially among the youth. Another reason is to prevent dangerous growth of social inequalities. Poverty and exclusion is not going to coexist with growing wealth and conspicuous consumption of the elite. All those arguments point to the necessity to decrease the income gap through a system of progressive taxation. Funds acquired from raised tax revenues will serve to finance public spending.

Opportunities for the Polish Sectoral Policy and Dani Rodrik's Trilemma

Until recently, mainstream economists, politicians subscribing to their views and the influential media, sneered at the postulate for the public sector to finance the programs of fostering professional activity. This changed after the crisis began. Today, the public is aware of the enormous scale of the income gap and how it has increased over the entire era of neoliberalism and the development of its version of deregulated capitalism, beginning in the mid-1970s. Actually, the growth of this gap did not even cease during the crisis. Societies are more and more aware of the consequences of the interplay between political and financial elites, for example, the career change of a business people to being political representatives, extensive lobbying activities, etc. Relations between the world of politics and business favour the protection of high-income earners from redistribution – protection applied in the name of supporting economic growth, which is simply not true.

The awareness of this relationship is a necessary pre-condition of any change. Yet, this only forms an initial step toward such a transformation. While that awareness gave rise to the outraged (indigenous) movement, in this context it has not had a real significance apart from its effect in the media. The most serious problems hindering potential changes originate from the scale of international economic integration, from financialisation of the global economy and from the already mentioned golden straitjacket (see Orhangazi, 2008A, 2008B, Gomez and Korine, 2008, and Bresser-Pereira 2010).

Under conditions of free movement of capital, any attempt to enforce increased income taxes on groups of high income-earners may result in their flight. Worse still, the problem is not only about potential taxpayer flight or – in the case of entities operating in monopolistic positions – about transferring increased taxes onto their customers. Rodrik's "trilemma" illustrates this issue below.

Figure 2.1: Rodrik's trilemma.

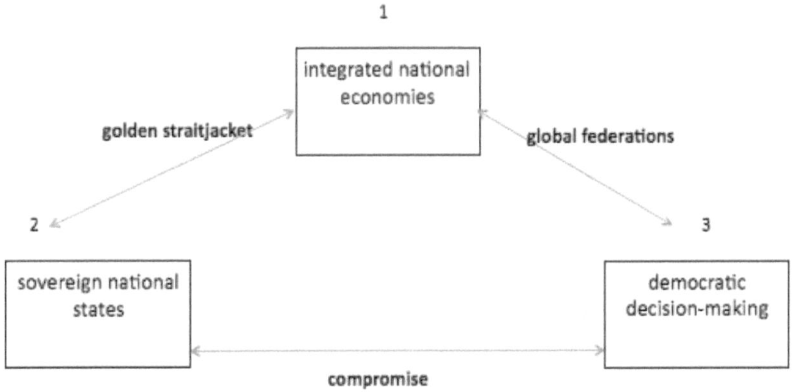

Source: Based on Rodrik (2011: 265).

In a similar vein but not referring to the same problem Obstfeld and Taylor define the open economy "trilemma" (Obstfeld and Taylor, 2002, 2004; Obstfeld, Shambaugh and Taylor, 2004, 2005, 2010) as the impossible trinity society faces: (1) international capital mobility; (2) fixed, state-regulated currency exchange rate; (3) the government's autonomous monetary policy. It is only possible for two of the three elements to coexist. For instance, in a given country, there exists international capital mobility (1), then it may enjoy only one of the two choices: either the freedom to regulate the currency exchange rate (2) or that of running the monetary policy (3). In the case policy makers are interested in, if a country's government has the freedom to regulate the exchange rate and run free monetary policy at the same time, then they will have to give up the freedom of capital movement.

In Rodrik's trilemma quite a similar rule applies. If we belong to an integrated global economy (1) and we maintain sovereign national state (2), then we must not expect that decisions concerning the economy would be made in line with procedures of democratic decision-making performed domestically (3). The choices, instead, are dictated by a "global federation" which, while not existing officially, is formed by capital markets and by international institutions of which we are members (such as the International Monetary Fund or the World Bank).

In light of this "trilemma," the taxpayers' freedom to flee from a "greedy government" is neither the only nor the most serious problem hindering raising the tax burdens of the wealthiest. What is also important in this context is the opinion of such a "federation" – i.e. of financial markets – about the government concerned as decision maker.

In fact, governments may be and indeed are punished for their "bad manners" with respect to financial elites, as well as they are for profligacy and insufficient saving. Quite a painful punishment administered for such attempts is the refusal of investment funds to finance the public debt, which in consequence may force a government to resign. The same applies to countries that are not seriously in debt. This type of dependency of sovereign national states on the way markets behave will prevent the redistribution of income in these countries and increase the financialisation of their economies.

However, it is possible, through interpretation of the Rodrik "trilemma," to find opportunities for a change. The golden straitjacket is probably going to become too tight over time and governing elites will not accept judgments of international markets as humbly as they accept them today.

Writing about the restricted access to political decisions at the national level, Rodrik quotes an analogy from the era of the gold standard adopted in various counties:

> *During the peak years of the gold standard a restricted domain of national policy (with its reliance upon the elites, so typical of it) ensured that domestic monetary policy could be even entirely subordinated to the need to maintain the gold parity. During the interwar period, when voting rights were extended to nearly everybody and workers managed to organise themselves, national governments found that it became no longer viable to maintain the economic orthodoxy of the gold standard. As the needs of full employment clashed with the need of the gold standard, it was the latter one that let go.* (Rodrik 2011:268)

The above-quoted example is a warning given to the fate of international integration and globalised economy – since we know what came after the gold standard era ended. If a partial dissolution of the Bretton Woods system was not dangerous, it was, perhaps, due to the "benevolent hegemony" of the United States and of the US Dollar (see Hellainer 2011:268). The New Deal, rather than on gold, depended on market trust in the US and its currency. In our case, we envision the possibility to overcome the limitations of the trilemma not through a workers' riot or violent manifestations of the outraged, but through a revolt of the governing elite. This revolt will pave the way to introduce new international arrangements and some sort of a reasonable compromise to restrict the dictate of markets.

If a progressive tax system will help the reinforcement of public finance and, at the same time, the reduction in the income gap, the role of indirect taxes should also be mentioned. The rise in living standard of societies – with smaller demand for non-renewable natural resources and less degradation to the environment – may depend on indirect taxes imposed on consumption.

The increases of the value added tax (VAT) and other indirect taxes we are witnessing now in individual countries are another manifestation of the golden straitjacket or simply, the opportunism of those in power who choose to raise this tax, which is politically easier to increase. However, reducing real income and lowering consumer demand of the substantially less wealthy part of society undercuts the recovery of the economy and deepens income stratification.

Conclusions

The issue that gives rise to the most controversy is the role of the nation state and its policy. The above-presented considerations indicate the need to increase the role of the government in the economy. We are aware of both the strengths and weaknesses of the small state concept, just as we are of the virtues and vices of the free market. Although excessively bureaucratic and omnipotent government is admittedly undesirable, so is a totally free market. Nobody has managed so far to codify the rules of a state at a happy medium. Francis Fukuyama (Stasiński 2012), usually bold in his opinions about the present and the future, says that it is necessary to rethink the State, but without offering a specific solution.

Before the present crisis, the market had too much power. By now, it has become evident that the deregulating, privatising, and shrinking of the role of the State, while market forces become more dominant, is a trend that should be reversed. Nevertheless, the return of the state needs control, too. This is the task for public opinion, including – perhaps more than anything else – the inputs of political economists and perhaps some management experts.

Bibliography

Albert M. (1993), *Capitalism Against Capitalism*. London: Whurr.

Albert M., Gonenc R. (1996), "The Future of Rhenish Capitalism", *Political Quarterly*, 67, (3): 184–193.

Baumol, W. J.; Tobin, J. (1989), "The Optimal Cash Balance Proposition: Maurice Allais' Priority", *Journal of Economic Literature* 27(3).

Bresser-Pereira, Luiz Carlos (2010), "The Global Financial Crisis and a New Capitalism?", Levy Economics Institute Working Paper No. 592.

Buras P. (2012), "Ulica zmieni świat" (The Street Will Change the World. An Interview with Wolfgang Streeck), *Gazeta Wyborcza*, 5–6 May.

Gomez P. Y. And *Korine H.* (2008), *Entrepreneurs and Democracy: A Political Theory of Corporate Governance*, Cambridge, UK: Cambridge University Press.

Hall P. A.; Soskice, David W (2001), *Varieties of Capitalism: the Institutional Foundations of Comparative Advantage*, Oxford: Oxford University Press.

Hellainer E. (2011), *Globalne ekonomie polityczne* (*Global Political Economies*), Kraków: Jagiellonian University Publishing.

Mankin N.G., Taylor M.P. (2009), *Mikroekonomia* (*Microeconomy*), Warsaw: PWE.

Mess H. (2012), *Choroba niskich stóp* (*The Disease of Low Rates*), "Forum", No. 13.

Obstfeld M., Shambaugh J., Taylor, A. (2004), "Monetary Sovereignty, Exchange Rates, and Capital Controls: The Trilemma in the Interwar Period," IMF Staff Papers51 (2004): 75–108.

Obstfeld M., Shambaugh J., Taylor, A. (2005), "The Trilemma in History: Tradeoffs among Exchange Rates, Monetary Policies, and Capital Mobility," *Review of Economics and Statistics*, 87.3 (August): 423–438.

Obstfeld M., Shambaugh J., Taylor A. (2010), "Financial Stability, the Trilemma, and International Reserves," *American Economic Journal: Macroeconomics*, 2.2 (April): 57–94.

Obstfeld, M., Taylor, A. (2002), "Globalization and Capital Markets," *National Bureau of Economic Research Working Paper* 8846, March.

Obstfeld,M., Taylor A. (2004), *Global Capital Markets: Integration, Crisis, and Growth*, New York and Melbourne: Cambridge University Press, 2004.

Orhangazi O. (2008A), *Financialisation and the US Economy*, Edward Elgar Publishing.

Orhangazi O. (2008B), "Financialisation and Capital Accumulation in the Nonfinancial Corporate Sector: A Theoretical and Empirical Investigation on the US Economy, 1973–2003", *Cambridge Journal of Economics*, 32(6): 863–886.

Ratajczak M. (2012), "Finansyzacja gospodarki" (Financialisation of economy), *Ekonomista*, No. 3.

Rifkin J. (2003), *Koniec pracy. Schyłek siły roboczej na świecie i początek ery postrynkowej* (*The end of labour. The Decline of labour Worldwide and the Beginning of the Post-Market Era*), Wrocław: Wydawnictwo Dolnośląskie.

Rodrik D. (2011), *Jedna ekonomia, wiele recept* (*One economy, many recipes*), Warsaw: Wydawnictwo Krytyki Politycznej.

Stasiński M. (2012), "Państwo sztywne jak fabryka Forda" (The State as Rigid as a Ford factory. An interview with Francis Fukuyama), *Gazeta Wyborcza*, 2–3 June.

Strange S. (1996), *Casino Capitalism*, Oxford: Basil Blackwell.

Watson, P. (2012), "Sackings Expose the Harsh Reality of Poland's Junk Jobs", *The Guardian*, 23 July, available at: http://www.theguardian.com/commentisfree/2012/jul/23/sackings-poland-junk-jobs-chung-hong; accessed on August 23, 2013.

Williamson J.(1989), "What Washington Means by Policy Reform", in: Williamson J. (ed.): *Latin American Readjustment: How Much has Happened*, Washington: Institute for International Economics.

Alojzy. Z. Nowak,
Kazimierz Ryć

Capability of Convergence as Imperative for Euro Area Persistence

Introduction

The economy of Euro area member states struggles to overcome the recession that followed the most recent crisis. The crisis neither originated from the Euro area nor even from Europe as a whole. However, as it reached the Euro area, its impact turned out to be quite devastating. A majority of Euro area countries have since then recorded GDP at levels vastly lower than their potential suggests, in some cases even lower than the levels seen prior to the crisis. Countries of Southern Europe with their relatively poorer levels of development were most seriously affected – ironically, it was that group of countries which had hoped to quicken the rates of their development within the Euro area, expecting benefits to be enjoyed in the wake of adoption of the common currency. Economic tensions also resulted in aggravating political disputes. Voices were heard heralding the decline of the Euro area while the ranks of Euro-sceptical politicians and experts augmented, including economists previously in favour of the common currency. While the sheer number of Euro area member states keeps increasing, other EU countries, in particular larger ones, experience visibly shrinking enthusiasm for their accession. It seems that political arguments started prevailing over economic ones in their respective debates upon the accession. The Economic and Monetary Union – the entity we shortly refer to as the Euro area – is thus undergoing profound changes. Let us then consider some of these changes and their underlying conditions.

Mechanism of Convergence and Free Market

The establishment of a common currency in the Euro Area was supposed to foster economic growth of less developed countries, mainly those situated in the southern part of Europe. The operation of the convergence mechanism, on the other hand, was to emerge from free market forces. Less developed countries had comparative advantages in the form of lower wages, larger labour force, resources, and lower capitalisation. This summed up to quite a beneficial situation:

- Cheap and unused resources of production factors from the South;
- Abundance of capital from the northern Euro Area countries;
- Low interest rates and readily available credit.

These factors would accelerate the rate of economic growth in less developed countries and, over time, it was hoped, would lead to equalisation of GDP levels throughout the zone. Of course, countries of the wealthy North were also expected to benefit from faster growth of the South.

Unfortunately, these hopes have not been realised. The invisible hand of the free market has mismanaged investments as additional streams of capital flow have surged. Instead of much desirable convergence, what followed was actually divergence (which still goes on). The economies of the southern states have become uncompetitive in comparison with the northern Europe member states and their global trade partners. This is partly due to higher Euro exchange rates, shaped by the economically sound North, but being "too high" for the southerners.

Several problems affect the shortfall in real convergence:

- Abundant capital inflow from the North, accompanied by scarce inflow of foreign direct investments;
- Relatively meagre increase of direct trade exchange within the Euro Area;
- Many investments missing the mark, financed with credit originating from capital inflow and directed into sectors subject to speculative bubbles, such as in Spain and Ireland (real estate bubbles in particular);
- Cheap financing of public debt increases with low Euros interest rates, for example, Greece, Portugal, and Italy;
- Increasing labour costs in terms of goods and non-tradable services, which resulted in the Balassa-Samuelson effect – growth of inflation in some cases,
- The strengthening Euro exchange rate led to loss of competitiveness compared to other trade partners,
- Open global economy, which is beneficial for the wealthy northern part of the Euro Area, proved disastrous for the South,
- Southern part of the zone suffered from deindustrialisation.

The last point above is due to the fact that investment, which has been financed by capital inflow from the North, ended up largely in the South in the non-tradable sector, while the tradable good sector could not compete with the leading manufacturers from the North and the cheap producers from Eastern Europe.

Macroeconomic problems caused by this process of divergence were disguised under the scope of generally sound business practices at micro level. However, the recent global crisis unravelled the real scale of the macro effects on the southern economies. From the crisis, which hit in the years of 2007–2009, there has been no recovery despite some symptoms of rebound.

The need to bail out the banking system using government funds clearly evidenced the weakness of economy in the southern countries. Public debt has soared, as did the level of indebtedness to creditors from the northern countries. George Soros described the situation that emerged quite brutally, but aptly all the same. In his opinion, at the beginning, the European Union was meant to be a voluntary association of equal states, which sacrificed some of their sovereignty for the sake of a common benefit. However, he argues that the crisis of the Euro Area turned into a union of unequal states divided into debtors and creditors where the latter countries have the power to dictate economics policies.

The relationship between debtors and creditors reflects the essence of dependence between weak and strong economies. Additionally, high public debt undermines debtors' position and lead to cuts is government expenditures, thereby in turn to a deflation of aggregate demand in the debtor economy and so to lower tax proceeds and so potentially to irresolution of the initial public debt problem. Economies like Germany with its strong tradable goods sector and much less debt drag are able to maintain their economies growth by increasing their exports, which compensates for decreased domestic demand in the slowdown period. In contrast, the debtors tend to suffer from uncompetitive export goods sectors, low GDP, increased unemployment, and of debt increase (*inter alia* the effect of higher interest rates paid in the bond market).

Floating Exchange Rate Bad – Euro Better?

Before the Euro was established and adopted as the common currency, there was a great deal of argument in scholarly discussions and political debates about the advantages of the Euro and economic benefits expected to stem from it. What few people highlighted at that time were the weaknesses of a floating exchange rate system – the one that the common currency was going to replace in trade and financial operations within the Euro area. It is quite understandable that more attention is paid to an emerging project than to one becoming a thing of the past. Today, on the other hand, many economists not only nostalgically remember the strengths of the system abandoned within the Euro area but actually go as far as postulate a reversion to floating exchange rates. What we are postulating, instead, is to keep very sober and reserved in this respect.

To put it brutally the floating exchange rate system leads to unpredictability in the short run and maladjustment in the long run.

Firstly, the floating rate is a rather hazardous instrument of competitive rivalry within any economic community as it creates temptation for a country to manipulate with monetary policy in order to achieve depreciation of its domestic currency in relation to currencies of its trade partners. J. M. Keynes was quite explicit in calling such a practice an attempt to export unemployment. In order to prevent and control this in the Single Market before the Euro institution, the so-called currency snake was introduced (1971–1976), with poor results; and later (with somewhat better results despite a major crisis in 1992) the European Monetary System EMS (1979–1999).

Secondly, as a floating exchange rate makes it easier – through depreciation – to achieve an external balance thanks to making exports cheaper and imports more expensive, it ends up pre-justifying and really absolving the lack of competitiveness, and it fails to impose necessary real adjustments and innovativeness of production and of the export offer. The currency depreciation is just a palliative rather than real curative medicine to poor economy competitiveness. It anaesthetises more than it cures. In this sense it may only be helpful as a painkiller at a stage when a country puts much effort to achieve structural adjustment. After all, it was for this purpose that devaluations were applied under the Bretton Woods fixed exchange rate system – the ones Paul Volcker refers to as fixed exchange rates subject to adjustments.[1]

Thirdly, floating exchange rate enables overtly pragmatic or even opportunistic state authorities to avoid (or at least postpone) burdensome decisions about economic modernisation. Depreciation of a currency may, as a result, actually become a continuous process, lowering a developing country's rate of growth that exposes it to a risk of falling into the stagnant middle-income trap.

Fourthly, under conditions of globalisation and financialisation of the global economy, the floating exchange rate becomes entirely unpredictable, in particular for a small open economy. As aptly shown by Hélène Rey,[2] a the notorious trilemma faced by monetary and exchange rate policy under circumstances of free movement of capital turns into a simpler dilemma – namely, it becomes an alternative: either the free movement of capital or the sovereignty of monetary policy – which, in fact, deprives a small open economy of the latter factor, that of the sovereignty, because it is hardly possible to establish any effective barrier to capital movement.

1 *Obserwator Finansowy*, 25 July 2014.

2 Rey H., "The Emergence of the Euro as an International Currency", in: Portes R., *Economic Policy*, 26 April 1998.

And it is only fifthly that a number of serious inconveniences to trade and international business such as transactions costs and foreign exchange risks may be mentioned in relation to the floating exchange rate. These rather than the points made above had been mainly emphasised before the Euro introduction and indeed the common currency has managed very effectively to eliminate them on all intra-Euro area transactions.

The common currency of the European Union members intended to prevent negative consequences of dissolution of the Bretton Woods system. Under floating exchange rates countries are eager to adjust their monetary policies to achieve depreciation of their domestic currency, thereby rendering their exports more competitive and enjoying positive current accounts balance. The system of Bretton Woods and the gold standard became popular thanks to their control of such monetary policies. The gold standard excluded the exchange rate-related policies from the macroeconomic policy toolkit. A country's economy depended upon external balances, which were necessary to retain fixed rates. Difficulties with maintenance of the fixed exchange rates necessitate the implementation of deflation policy whenever a deficit in current counts emerged under the gold standard. The harsh consequences of such a policy tends usually to affect unequally different social groups.

Financial support can enable them to apply solutions for emerging social problems. To be sure, the relation between money and gold can lead to political hegemony by countries with significant gold stocks (the US under Bretton Woods for example).

The Bretton Woods system did the job in practice. However, it was politically costly and it had not entirely done away with devaluation, which could still be used in situations of fundamental disequilibrium. It was thus an adjustable peg system of fixed exchange rates. Eventually severe turbulence in the global economy in the early 1970's led to the dissolution of the Bretton Woods system and brought a gradual revival of flexible exchange rates. In fact, flexible exchange rates seemed attractive options for politicians allowing them to conduct apparently independent national monetary policy.

Flexible exchange rates allow politicians also to avoid unpopular decisions. Where depreciation of domestic currency occurred, entailing consequences related with inflation, it was easy to blame financial markets and remain clean. Governments influence currency exchange rates by using monetary policies. This intervention came to be increasingly contested by conservative economists. Under the influence of the theory of rational expectations that justified the idea of limited effectiveness of governments' intervention in the economy the now fully independent central banks in many developed countries targeted inflation rates and strove for price stability above all. As a consequence, exchange rate policies and external trade balance were entrusted to market-based mechanisms. In short, central banks were entrusted to maintain price stability while market mechanism was expected to do all the rest.

In theory, the system of flexible exchange rates combined with central banks' inflation target policy should ensure smooth operation of markets. Reality however, proved otherwise. Neither did the currencies' exchange rates fit the economy fundamentals nor did the achievement of an inflation target ensure a balance in the economy. The financial crisis of 2008–2010 reveals the latter problem. Actually, the flawed nature of flexible exchange rate systems under conditions of globalisation and financialisation had appeared earlier.

In particular flexible exchange rates became a barrier to further economic integration in the European Union and a serious reason to give up national currencies and create the common currency – *the Euro*. Obviously, there were other reasons. They notably included political considerations with further economic integration seen as a further step towards the "ever closer union among the peoples of Europe" envisaged by the Rome Treaty and a profound desire to counter the continuing hegemony of the US Dollar as a currency for international transactions of all kinds.

In debates held during the stage of deepening globalisation, proponents of the introduction of the Euro pointed out many expected benefits to be enjoyed by the entire global economy. The Euro fits perfectly within the concepts of trade liberalisation and international cooperation. It also influences the operations of individual national economies. It was not only liberals that could expect the common currency to render more flexible prices and wages. The hope was that adopting the Euro will lead to improved competitiveness achieved through real adaptations of sound economic policies rather than through monetary manipulation undertaken in order to achieve lower exchange rate for domestic currency or through official devaluation.

This in fact signified the return to the ultraliberal neoclassical ideas of the gold standard. Free movement of goods, services, and capital, along with benefits brought also the rule of financial markets over politics. Financial markets, in line with the ultraliberal doctrine or ideology, are able to exercise a control over a number of governments' "non-rational" decisions. The most significant example is the abandonment by many governments of the instrument of industrial policy and disregard for the role of industry in GDP in favour of services. Today, this error (mainly in Spain, Greece) means millions of people out of work. Now, many governments in the EU are beginning to understand better the need to rebuild or innovate in some neglected sectors of the real economy.

All the above-mentioned circumstances have to be recognised as one analyses the possibility of restoring debtor countries' competitive edge. In particular sectoral industrial policy surely has a central role to play in this context, and implies a return to what Roosevelt called a "socially-rooted" liberalism and what in Europe has been known as the indicative planning of the Social Market Economy.

Proposals for Repairing the Monetary Union's Operation

One might distinguish two interpretations of the reasons for the crisis of the Monetary Union in the Eurozone. First, some governments are irresponsible for allowing an excessive growth of public and/or private sectors indebtedness. Consequences of this indebtedness were painfully exposed by the crisis. As a result, countries ruled by irresponsible politicians lost the confidence of the financial markets. Second, the Euro system has several flaws in its structure and implementation. These flaws remained partly hidden over the period of good business outlooks. This reason is lent supportive arguments by many sceptics of implementing the Euro Area project in the first place. Many American economists and some academic circles in Europe share this opinion.[3]

Germans and other economists representing the neoliberal economy uphold the first interpretation above. The Belgian economist Paul De Grauwe points out that less developed Euro Area countries have no real control over the currency in which they become indebted. This exposes them to uncontrolled inflows or outflows of capital streams, depending on the changing confidence that financial markets accord to them. Under such conditions, they are unable to manage their liquidity since they do not control the money supply. This threatens to provoke a financial crisis even where no fundamental reasons are present.[4]

According to the "German interpretation," the remedy to heal the system is to restore trust in the indebted countries through reduction (some may go as far as elimination) of its budgetary deficit, gradual decrease of its public debt, and improvement of competitiveness through reduced production costs. This strategy requires stricter EU surveillance over economic and budgetary policy as under the Stability and Growth Pact as well as upon new instruments counteracting

---

3 Dornbusch R., *Keys to Prosperity: Free Markets Sound Money and a Bit of Luck*, Cambridge: MIT Press, 2000.

4 De Grauwe P., *Prospects for Monetary Unions after the Euro*, Cambridge: The MIT Press, 2005.

macroeconomic disproportions (the Fiscal Compact of 2013). Germans firmly emphasise introduction of the principle of fiscal discipline, which learning from the past experience should remain under strict control and be subject to financial sanctions whenever it is infringed.

The point of view shared by Germany and a couple of other states – recently turned creditor countries – is based upon a belief that over the last decades, significant differences emerged among EU member states with regards to the levels of competitiveness as well as excessive distortions of macroeconomic balance. Strong mutual economic links often resulted in negative phenomena occurring in other member states, thus weakening the resilience of the entire EU economy to external shocks. These factors impact the way the Economic and Monetary Union operates. According to this theory, this happened due to divergence and ignoring the provisions of the Stability and Growth Pact by some EU member states.

Therefore, according to proponents in order to eliminate the existing macroeconomic imbalances and counteract emergence of subsequent ones, a special mechanism for surveillance over the EU member states' macroeconomic condition is required. It relies on three fundamentals:

- Early warning system;
- Application of precisely defined rules, included in the Excessive Imbalance Procedure (EIP) and;
- Strict enforcement of the same, with financial sanctions imposed upon member states of Euro Area in cases of a breach.

As foreseen, the procedure of correcting actions will be launched when, based upon a detailed assessment of situation, the European Commission finds excessive macroeconomic imbalance in a given member state.[5] In such a case, the Council, instructed by the Commission, will have the right to adopt a recommendation stating the occurrence of such excessive imbalance. They can recommend a member state concerned to undertake necessary remedies (pursuant to Article 121(4) of the EU Treaty) and define a time frame within which such member state is obliged to present a plan for corrective measures, together with a schedule for implementation.

The Fiscal Compact thus adopted, also known as the "Six-Pack," (see Chapter 6) demands rigorous sanctions for chronic infringements by a member state to the

5 Regulation (EU) No. 1174/2011 of the European Parliament and of the Council of 16 November 2011 on enforcement measures to correct excessive macroeconomic imbalances in the euro area.

common currency area of the rules of the Stability and Growth Pact. It has become evident that efforts of several governments, especially in southern Europe, in applying the fiscal discipline required by the Six-Pack, are undeniable. Still, the evaluation of this policy is equivocal.

While the authors of this chapter share the idea of rationalisation of state expenditure, i.e. avoiding living beyond one's means, it recommends a new prescription for the problem of southern European countries. The German model is not the only basis upon which one may heal an economy. Germany has not the same experiences as Greece in terms of fiscal soundness, country size and export potential.

Actually, there is yet another conclusion to be drawn from German experiences, suggesting a possibility to reduce differences among Euro Area member states in terms of their competitiveness. This could be achieved by using internal income redistribution in the zone countries, considering that little room is left for external transfers given the size and nature of the EU Budget. If the reduction of labour costs is considered a recipe for improving the competitiveness of countries of the South, then it might be feasible to meet their endeavours halfway and increase real wages in the countries of the North. This postulate need not be regarded as an evidence of the authors' caustic attitude; rather, it should be seen as one ethical suggestion amid a range of moral challenges addressed at the EU outsiders. In the world as a whole considerations of equity point to a need to increase world real wage levels, not to drive them downwards in a "race to the bottom." It would be easier to achieve the same effect if Germany allows for a higher domestic inflation rather than in the weaker partner countries. In that case, price competitiveness, lost during the stage of price adjustments, as the Balassa-Samuelson effect in the Euro Area, would be restored. However, acceptance of higher inflation by Germany is admittedly unlikely.

Given this situation, we would favour a "semi-Keynesian" approach: it is postulated, first or at least in parallel, to use financial instruments to support the countries suffering from the crisis in order to enable them to stimulate economic growth and create jobs. The unused or under-used financial instruments one has in mind mainly include the following:

- Low-interest credits from the European Stability Mechanism (ESM),
- Loans from European Investment Bank,
- Increased investments in human capital,
- Further treasury bonds redemption by the European Central Bank,
- Banking regulations preventing the emergence of speculative bubbles;

- Eurobonds, that is to say, the issue of government bonds by the Euro – 18 borrowing together as a bloc – so far, just a proposal, Eurobonds are not implemented due to the lack of approval, mainly on the part of Germany. Eurobonds would lower the indebtedness costs of the peripheral southern countries, but would raise the costs for the largest Northern economies.

This kind of policy re-orientation, especially the final proposal requires a deep politico-economic integration and the establishment of a new model of solidarity within the European Union. Today, in practice the Community actions consists of a plodding implementation of the "German" option with only certain elements of the semi-Keynesian option, perhaps better described as a solidarity variant. We believe that the currently implemented policies may alleviate the effects of the crisis, but are still insufficient to eliminate the risk of dissolution of the Economic and Monetary Union. Their implementation is not going to eradicate the roots of tensions stemming from disillusioned hopes for real convergence, that is a gradual elimination of structural economic differences occurring among the European Union member states.

We also agree with Karol Lutkowski who highlighted considerable differences in levels of economic development from the very beginning, between the geographically central areas of the EU, and the Mediterranean and Atlantic peripheries. According to Lutkowski, these gaps are accompanied by divergent production structures. Development usually translated into shrinking of share of traditional sectors to the benefit of processing industry and the services sector. Differences of structures related with different development levels make for individual stages within any business cycle to occur asynchronously. This entails a threat to the common currency system due to asymmetric developments, depending on the stage of a cycle they face. The European Central Bank cannot satisfy each country while running policies of a uniform interest rate, oriented at maintenance of a certain, rather low but still averaged inflation for the entire Euro Area.

The problem is only going to be alleviated when gaps between development levels are significantly diminished, structures of production are more assimilated and intra-branch specialisation gains more importance. This is the "real convergence." It has better opportunities to proceed faster free from exchange-rate risk, i.e. within the common currency system. However, as long as this process is incomplete, the common currency is under risk of failure.[6]

6 Lutkowski K., "Co Się Stało w Strefie Euro?" (What happened in the Euro Area?), *Rzeczpospolita*, 15 June 2012.

Thus far, both the scope and types of remedy measures, although originating from opposing diagnoses about the reasons of the Euro crisis, count on more controlled and regulated markets to remedy the problem. We can also now cite the first attempts to evaluate the consequences of coordinated fiscal consolidation in the European Union member states. The International Monetary Fund, based on the work of the economists Barrell, Holland and Hurst (2012) on the National Institute Global Econometric Model (NIGEM) and upon data regarding the present crisis[7] arrive at the following key conclusions:[8]

- In "normal times" fiscal consolidation would lead to a decreased index of public indebtedness with respect to GDP in the EU member states, however in the present situation it is probably going to harm the entire European Union;
- Plans for fiscal consolidation as implemented today are going to lead to increase rather than decrease in the public debt in 2013 in relation to GDP in the entire EU;
- The same is going to happen in almost all individual EU member states (including the United Kingdom and where only Ireland is an exception);
- Coordinated programmes of budgetary cuts implemented in periods of dire economic straits actually cause contrary effects to those intended and thus are detrimental.

The above-mentioned three economists, whose data are used to draw conclusions about fiscal therapy in the EU, are convinced that the present tightening economic policies in many countries, in particular in southern Europe, are counterproductive. According to them:

1. Under normal circumstances one may expect that effects of more restrictive fiscal policy would be alleviated by loosened monetary policy. When monetary policy is liberalised, what follows is reduction of long-term interest rates. This stimulates investments and partially compensates the painful consequences of budgetary cuts. At present, however, interest rates are extremely low so any further sharpening of fiscal policy is probably not going to produce a compensatory reaction in monetary policy. While programs of so-called quantitative easing (money supply expansion) are implemented, as are those of loosening

---

7 Barrell, R., Holland, D. and Hurst, A.I. (2012), "Fiscal consolidation Part 2: fiscal multipliers and fiscal consolidations", OECD Economics Department Working Paper No. 933.

8 Report, *World Economic Outlook*, December 2012.

of credit policy, effects of these efforts are limited due to low interest on "risk-free assets."

2. Over the period of slowdown, i.e. a period of high unemployment and significant probability of losing a job, a larger share of households and enterprises struggle with decreased access to credit. In non-crisis periods, when perfect capital markets operate and consumers correctly anticipate the future, households are able to adequately distribute consumption over time. In such conditions, consumers' expenses are largely independent of the economy's condition at a given moment or on transitional shocks to fiscal policy. However, all these market reactions in normal times are not present during periods of severe economic downturns.
3. When all countries implement contractionary fiscal policies at the same time, production in each one of them not only becomes restricted but also – through trade and commercial links – causes contractions in other countries. In the case of the European Union the consequences of simultaneous budgetary cuts are serious, spreading recession throughout the entire Community's economic system.

Many today admit that the applications of shock therapy in the European Union as well as policies advocated by the International Monetary Fund have been a crucial mistake. Germany, which has tried to force the southern European countries, Greece in particular, to tighten their belts, should acknowledge that such a one-sided strategy has been erroneous.

We would incline to the view that radical governmental budgetary cuts are the wrong policy measures, although we do not argue that countries undergoing such a shock therapy are not at guilt. However, the history of successfully developed economies indicates the efficacy of policy not restricted to monetary and fiscal areas, but including also the real sphere of the economy and people's income and living standards. At the same time, we believe that while analysing the Single Market – the great achievement of the European Union – one should also take into account the issue of productivity and competitiveness of the weak economies within the market.

Labour Market Condition in the EU – Dilemmas and Challenges

The process of divergence of the Euro Area economies has already happened. However, this may proceed even further, considering that temporary competitive advantages of the northern countries are augmented by high credit cost in the Southern countries for governments, businesses, and households alike. The hindrance presented by increasing costs of credit, higher than in the North of the EU, diminishes the chances of Southern countries to compete in the Single Market.

For how long will debtors remain trapped in this trap? Is the economy enlivening, which is probably altering the present situation? It is difficult and troublesome to alleviate tensions occurring nowadays in the labour markets of these countries. Such tensions not only lead to social conflicts and unrest, but also undermine people's confidence in the sense of the hitherto-applied model of European integration.

In this context, the analysis of reasons underlying changes in the labour market is an important element in the dispute over the advisability of state intervention in the areas of employment and unemployment. Andrzej Wojtyna believes that "...where no immediate labour market compensation occurs, a room opens up for active macroeconomic policy." This author argues that limited wages flexibility prevents the private sector to react in the manner envisaged in neo-classical economic models. Where a government is able to adapt its policy sooner and react to a downturn more effectively, then, room appears for traditional Keynesian stimulation of demand.

Experts like Janusz Heller and Kamil Kotlinski provide interesting studies about the relationship between public finance and the unemployment level. They examined 15 Euro Area countries over the period 2000–2011 and conclude the following:

- Firstly, the application of mistaken fiscal policy leading to excessive state indebtedness during the financial distress of 2009–2011 resulted in negative consequences for individual Euro Area states. For instance, a group of countries with relatively stable public finance, such as Netherlands, Denmark, Finland and Sweden, which remains beyond the Euro Area, recorded increased unemployment rate in the years 2009–2011. The Authors emphasised that public finance stabilisation never precludes some forms of fiscal expansion, mainly those focus on maintaining low levels of unemployment. However, these countries had enough budgetary reserves to dampen the effects of negative crisis through a countercyclical fiscal policy. This enabled them to reduce the scale of increased unemployment.
- The Authors stated that countries with destabilised public finance reacted in various ways to the crisis. Greece and Portugal could not contain the accelerated increase in their unemployment rate. At the same time, these countries also recorded further deterioration of their destabilised public finance due to the costs of debt incurred. Greece and Portugal suffered from external shocks that

show their weaknesses. They could not counteract the negative consequences of the cited external shocks.

The conclusions from these studies lead to further analyses about the background of unemployment in the Euro Area. According to Grzegorz Tchorek, the factors improving the ability to react to and alleviate external shocks include the mobility of production factors and flexibility of prices and wages, although the government fiscal policy nevertheless plays a crucial role.[9] In his opinion, by applying an overly expansive fiscal policy over the period of relative stability, some countries of southern Europe and the Baltic regions depleted their ability to use fiscal policy instruments right at the time when the first external shocks emerged. Some of the answers to these problematic shocks include: serious and socially hurtful public expenditure savings, pressure upon the EU partners to lend a helping hand in the form of debt cuts or further credit facilitations.

The Need for a New Vision in the Area of Economic Policy

A deep diagnosis of the condition of the European Union is necessary in order to guarantee its survival (which is very desirable). Members of the Euro Area need fundamental changes in their economic policy. First, a more pronounced role is needed for sectoral policy, including industrial policy. In fact, it is only through active sectoral policy, implemented at both the level of the European Commission and the individual national countries, that the process of real convergence in the EU can generate a new stimulus.

Instead of being modelled upon old industrial policy, this sectorial policy needs to be a brand new sectoral policy relevant to times of integration. Such broadly understood policy is not entirely unfamiliar in the European Union. After all, it concerns the support, given thereby in various forms to such sectors as:

- Agriculture;
- Small and medium-sized enterprises start-ups;
- Infrastructure development;
- Education and human capital development;
- Support for a variety of initiatives in the areas of environment protection, culture, art, etc.

---

9 Tchorek G., "Teoretyczne podstawy integracji walutowej" (Theoretical Fundations of Monetary Integration), in: *Mechanizmy funkcjonowania strefy euro* (*Mechanisms of the Functioning of Eurozone*), Kowalewski P., Tchorek G., Górski J. (eds.), NBP, Warsaw, 2011.

All these efforts, perhaps, except for the first and the last categories, are aimed at supporting or correcting market-based mechanisms. Sectoral policy should fine-trim the operation of market mechanisms in individual economic sectors to increase employment rate, foster economic growth, foster specialisation and collaboration, and encourage higher equality. Such a policy could if suitably defined also protect the economy from the emergence of speculative bubbles. We do not think these are idealistic utopian solutions. It is possible, indeed necessary, to implement them.

Understood in this way, the sectoral policy is meant to direct the invisible hand of the market, using the visible hand of the government and with the collaborative hand of other EU member states. The target is real convergence. This can be done by targeting the areas that are crucial to stimulate the process of real convergence. Indeed, in the postulate of reverting the hitherto prevailing trend of divergence we see an essential opportunity for development of the European Union and Euro Area. This, we realise, is not going to be an easy task.

The crisis in Europe reveals that one has to deal with a serious and aggravating crisis of trust in the European Union, mistrust in both the individual politicians as well as in currently existing institutions. This is accompanied by decreasing trust in the idea of European solidarity, which has been developed since the end of World War 2 and has been a centrepiece of European integration. What looms and strengthens are national egoisms in Euro Area members, hindering further integration.

We believe however that there is an opportunity for the European Union to create a new vision based on a sectoral policy in which the visible hand replaces the invisible one. As mentioned above, we know many examples of effective sectoral policy, often under a simple name of industrial policy. The problem is the ideological barrier arising from the prevailing neoliberalism and the institutionalisation of pre-conditions imposed by the Economic and Monetary Union (EMU) and the World Trade Organisation (WTO).

According to typical variants of this ideology, the government usually has a dreadful reputation. State authorities are seen as lazy, cynical bureaucrats, afraid of doing anything non-schematic. Sometimes they are corrupt as well. Meanwhile, the opposite (private sector) side is perceived as hard working, dedicated entrepreneurs or private employers, and risks takers. The black, evil image of the former ones is false and simplified opposite to the white and innocent image of the latter ones. There are highly competent and reliable officers as well as greedy, egoistic, shortsighted executives, quick to commit fraud, and with the attitude of "grab the money and run."

First, the Euro Area countries should build quality institutions and fair competition. Second, there is not a single universal or best pattern for capitalism and the role of the government therein. The one regarded as universal is only the model preferred by the International Monetary Fund and by the financial markets.

One needs to be aware that it would not be easy to implement a proper sectoral policy within the present institutional system of the Economic and Monetary Union. However, this is crucial, if one advocates for the continuous development of the Euro Area. One must not overlook the trap into which some debtor countries have fallen. Resolving only the sovereign government debt problem, although necessary, is not going to restore or engender these countries' competitiveness.

At the same time, long-term unemployment is a social drama, especially for young people because it entails fatal consequences like hysteresis, migration, economic instability conditions and cavities in the nation's substance.

What is Sectoral Policy?

In order to improve competitiveness and economic growth, the following conditions are necessary:

- Promote the small and medium-sized (SME) enterprise sector. A particular emphasis should be given to promote SME "market discoveries."
- Develop the sector of businesses with prospects to generate high added value, innovative production or enjoying higher probabilities of increasing export;
- Create new jobs, mainly in the areas of goods but also in non-traded services, such as health service, child and elderly care, education, etc.

These proposals reveal some ideas of indicative planning, which, of course, remains inconsistent with strict neoliberal doctrines.

To rebuild their competitiveness, countries of southern Europe need to develop instruments and measures used by "emerging markets." This kind of approach is not easy to implement given the obligations resulting from membership in the EMU and agreements made under the WTO. Nonetheless one needs to be aware that free market-based mechanisms are ineffective in overcoming these problems, at least within a time frame acceptable to the present generation.

Today is the time to start testing the European Union institutions, agencies, and the banking system before implementing new sectoral (industrial) policies.

Productivity and Economic Competitiveness

We would argue that an increase in productivity is of general benefit only if it serves almost everybody and be distributed over all layers of society, indeed the entire international community. Competitiveness refers to somebody's advantage against someone else, usually to the other person's detriment For example, devaluation improves one country's competitiveness versus its trading partner(s). This, in turn, weakens the latter's competitiveness. For our partners, devaluation of our currency means appreciation of their currencies, potentially leading to retaliation in this or other manners, where eventually, all countries lose. In order to avoid monetary wars under the Bretton Woods system, devaluations were agreed through arbitration by the International Monetary Fund. Countries had the right to defend their current account balance in cases of fundamental exchange rate disequilibrium and their partners were likely to agree to such currency devaluations.

While building the Common Market, member states wanted to increase productivity and have indeed achieved this goal. The increase in productivity has been an impressive success. Member states were assisted in that attainment by the Bretton Woods system since they solved, sometimes better, sometimes not as soundly, the problems of competitiveness. When that system collapsed in the mid-70s, exchange rate battles in an effort to improve one country's competitiveness made it difficult to proceed with concordant cooperation among the Community partners. The Deutschmark could not replace the US Dollar nor could the Federal Republic of Germany stand in the US's shoes as "beneficial hegemony." This was not only due to historical residues or Germany's economic power, but also due to Germany's heavy reliance on exports and so on its export competitiveness.

But a problem that needs a solution is the non-competitiveness of a country within a common currency area. According to the neoliberal doctrine, when the free market fails, it is the fault of the State. That is what 189 Germans economists had in mind as they agitated to block the initiative of establishing the European Stability Mechanism (ESM). Instead of the collective support mechanism set up in 2012 that could be made permanent in a modified form from 2013, the economists argued it would be better to let countries restructure their debts. "Restructuring allows the countries concerned to reduce their debt and start again," said the economists. However, ultimately the German Federal Constitutional Court ruled that Germany may ratify the Treaty on the ESM, if their financial responsibility in this respect shall not exceed the agreed 190 billion Euros.[10]

10 Judgment of The Federal Constitutional Court – Second Senate, September 12, 2012.

Irresponsible governments should pay for their misconduct. At the same time, it not appropriate to deprive countries the right of self-defence in cases of fundamental imbalance. By becoming member states of the European Union, countries were obligated to adopt the common currency, but while renouncing any possibility of self-defence adjustment measures. Should the European Stability Mechanism play the role of an aid fund handing out charity money? The attitude of those who protested could be understandable as an earnest care for their own and their compatriots' interest, indeed survival. However, it is recommended that the Community institutions play an intermediary role in agreeing with some protectionist actions in cases where fundamental imbalance emerges. For example, the Community could support re-industrialisation of southern European countries or similar efforts within sectoral policy.

This is where a question may be asked: what is the purpose of the Common, Single Market, if protectionism is still admissible? It should be emphasised that the Common Market is not a pure free market, as manifested by a range of existing regulations concerning its operation. It is not possible to eliminate all elements of protection because this is a common market. Hence what is crucial is rather that all the countries participating in the common market should have equal opportunities, or as is often said, should compete on a level playing field. This, in turn, leads to a hotly disputed debate as to how to define the institution and role of fair or non-distortive government aid in the European Union. According to the official definition unfair government aid is any intervention by state institutions consisting of providing, in any form, aid to either a single business entity or a group of businesses, which results in interference in the functioning of free markets.

Accordingly, any kind of aid accorded under the conditions noted below would be regarded as an illicit public aid:

a) An entrepreneur in functional understanding of this word, who is beneficiary of any kind of government support at start-up;
b) Aid that is provided through or from government sources in any form;
c) Aid that is selective and becomes to its beneficiary's benefit;
d) Anything that hinders competition by favouring some entrepreneurs;
e) Anything that influences trade exchange between the European Union member states.

Rules concerning government aid tend to be selective. Thus, licenses are granted to some entities to conduct business activities but are denied to other similar enterprises. Also very common is the prohibition of providing public services by a national or regional government on the basis of a contract made beyond the public procurement law.

All the above-mentioned reasons for providing government aid could seem to be justified in the current conjuncture of the European Union. The problem is that there are regulations in the Single Market, which undermine these principles. However in some cases, the European Commission approves various privileges and aids to companies or individual entrepreneurs, based upon some superior, valid social or economic reasons.

The European Union may approve government aid that covers, among others, areas such as:

- Regional policy,
- Investment activities aiming at increased employment in small and medium-sized enterprises,
- Aid to women's entrepreneurship,
- Activities for environmental protection,
- Support for advisory services in SME, their participation in training of fairs.

These are just a few examples of government aid provided by countries with approval from the European Commission.

We are convinced that these postulates call for more openness and agreement with regards to supporting business entities and entrepreneurs with the aim of improving their competitiveness. We need to underline that consent given to governments' efforts to improve competitiveness is, essentially, the same as consent given to devaluation. It might be more difficult to negotiate, but should be added to the arsenal of instruments and measures for the so-called "real devaluation" as a tool which is less painful to the society than neoclassical market adjustments through unemployment and wage and price deflation and at the same time, in our opinion, even more effective.

What is the Architecture that Better Fits the European Union?

This section considers the appropriate architecture for European Union and its priorities. The British Prime Minister David Cameron asked the question: which integration are we going to adopt: integration involving common currency or Common Market? In fact, both variants of integrations seem acceptable. We would hold that the case for economic integration is beyond doubt. Today, however, the key issue is the healing of the situation in the Euro Area. As important as this is for the Union itself, this is also crucial for the global market, which truly needs the Euro as one of the world's major currencies.

We share the view about the need to restore stability in the EU financial sector, although the task is not easy considering how interrelated this is with the budgetary condition of many countries. After the experience learned thus far, a common mechanism of surveillance of the European financial sector should act as guarantor of its stability. Therefore, the Banking Union seems a project, which should be approved in principle. Another disintegration of the European financial sector would entail a serious reduction in the scale of operations of the common European interbank market. This would constitute a major drawback to the entire real sector of the economy. The European Central Bank (ECB) controlled the liquidity of inter-bank clearance between countries of the southern and northern Europe due to its intervention. Experience gathered from the EU's financial market calls for strengthening, coordinating, and regulating the role of the ECB. However, the life buoy provided by the European Central Bank is no longer sufficient. Thus, the draft of the Banking Union, which actually goes much further than the establishment of new regulations for the ECB, needs to be fully implemented.

From the Polish point of view, the idea of Banking Union and the solutions to be adopted are important because Poland is probably going to become a member of the Euro Area. We perceive the Banking Union as a possibility of institutional support for the sake of increased productivity and competitiveness of the economies of the European Union. It may also be assumed that changes in the system of regulations and activities within the European banking system will make it possible to overcome the crisis of trust in financial markets. While not overestimating this argument, we also know that unregulated financial markets often tend to become a hardly acceptable compass for economic decisions and social policy (due for example to asset price bubbles and the like). However, they cannot be ignored. The only thing that should be avoided is an uncontrolled disruption of the Euro Area.

Poland and Euro Area

A majority of those involved in debates on the Polish economy agree that this is not the right time to enter the Euro Area. Differences appear around more detailed questions: whether to opt for the accession at all and when?

Not to tend to accession. Instead, to maintain liquid exchange rate of Polish Zloty, because sovereign monetary policy, which is possible in that case, is the one that serves best to sustainable economic growth. This argument is supported by other arguments such as that close economic cooperation with an enormous economic organism protects countries from excessive fluctuation of exchange rates in any case. However, monetary sovereignty is costly. Transaction costs are higher, as are costs of credit and of debt servicing, as well as all sorts of other costs and risks. In fact, other costs and risks were exposed by the present crisis and by the increasing consequences of global economic financialisation. Under the latter circumstances, exchange rates become divorced from actual condition of economies. Meanwhile, the common trilemma: free movement of capital – freedom of monetary policy – freedom of shaping the currency exchange rate, turns into a dilemma, and actually has an alternative: the free movement of capital or freedom of monetary policy and exchange rate policy.

Even if today this tearing of currencies exchange rates apart from the real sphere is not total, and the above-mentioned alternative is not omnipresent yet, the trend in this direction is evident. A small open economy loses its monetary and exchange rate sovereignty at the same time.[11] Possibilities of limiting the freedom of capital movement by governments are uncertain, while ways and means to evade such restrictions are aplenty. Finally, we do not really share the argument that extensive trade with a strong commercial partner contributes to stabilising the exchange rate of a small open economy's currency, in the sense that this gives a chance for Polish Zloty the to take advantage of an umbrella given by the Euro. In our opinion, this is only a temporary advantage to be enjoyed until the markets say: "let's check, then." Polish Zloty has already experienced the effects of such checking when, over a short period, the price of the US Dollar began to oscillate within the range between PLN 2 and 4. Poland's national economy suffered the impoverishment of households indebted in foreign currencies and of certain businesses, either similarly indebted or losing heavily on currency options.

- The most common opinion in Poland is that it is best to wait and see, observing changes occurring in the Euro Area, in order to decide about potential accession as a proper window of opportunity presents itself. Another variant of that strategy proposes to wait "with a loaded gun," i.e. to meet the Maastricht criteria and then to wait in readiness for the final decision. However, even if it costs nothing, this may entail a loss for both Poland and the European Union. Of course, it is desirable to meet the criteria, but this should be done calmly in order not to harm the present modest rate of growth.
- The best solution for Poland is to wait actively with participation. Poland is obliged to accession to Euro Area once ready and in any case it does not contest the benefits of a common currency. A strong European Union is beneficial to Poland and the global economy, once it regains its ability to act efficiently. It is just as important to Poland – bearing in mind the negative consequences

11 Rey H., "The Emergence of the Euro as an International Currency", in: Portes R., *Economic Policy*, 26 April 1998.

of such events – to prevent a collapse and in effect uncontrolled disruption of the Euro Area. The status of a country that is a candidate to accession enables Poland to actively participate in improving that Community and obliges it at the same time to bear the costs this involves.

Our Idea for Europe

We are arguing in effect, that there is still time for a solution based on a more active state interventionism, which is less revolutionary than total dissolution of the euro and partially an alternative to the mainstream of changes occurring nowadays in the Euro Area.

It should be observed, that at present it would be impossible to find political consensus for a process of return to national currencies, no matter how cleverly devised. After all almost all political forces along the Rhine share Germany's fears that the return to national currencies would entail appreciation of the Deutschmark, with all its potential consequences.

If there is something we are concerned about, it is that reforms made thus far, featuring an evident domination of fiscal solutions, may expose Europe to long-standing political conflicts and social unrest. This is deepening rather than decreasing productivity and competitiveness differences as between many Euro Area countries. If this bleak scenario comes true, Europe's position would become even weaker with respect to such global powers as USA, India, China or, recently, Mexico and Brazil.

Conclusions

In our opinion, the hitherto-existing fiscal approach should certainly be supplemented by solutions found and prepared for a new approach, which may be called *Keynesian.* Concerning a new role and importance of Brussels in the European Union, we observe, without being shocked or upset about it, that the need is increasing for Brussels' visible hand in order to overcome the crisis. However, our expectations from Brussels are more diversified and somehow different from those formulated by the mainstream remedies offered thus far. We welcome the European Commission's decision with regards to enlivening the labour market through an injection of the EU's structural funds. We also favour the news that the European Commission recently loosened financial discipline for six countries, including Poland, in order for them to catch a breath over a year or two before they make difficult reforms.

We essentially want to advocate to the European Union's politicians and decision-makers: the strategy to improve competitiveness and accelerate a socio-economic transformation. We claim that growth should include a combination and a dynamic continuation of efforts aimed at support to sectors of the economy. Then, a new vision is also needed in the area of economic policy. An active and well-defined role of the State will not only not hinder but in fact will help in over coming the serious, and socially dramatic economic situation experienced by many countries. The new priority for the European Union is therefore a strategy of par excellence economic nature that is taking seriously social values at the same time, while it encourages the acceleration of real convergence of the Euro Area member states. We reckon the assumptions of nominal convergence, are a strategy not ambitious and not productive enough to generate optimism unto the Euro Area and its future fate.

Bibliography

Dornbusch R. (2000), *Keys to Prosperity: Free Markets Sound Money and a Bit of Luck*, Cambridge: The MIT Press.

De Grauwe, P. (2009), *Economics of Monetary Union*, Oxford: Oxford University Press.

De Grauwe P. (2005), *Prospects for Monetary Unions after the Euro*, Cambridge: The MIT Press.

Helleiner E. (1996), *States and the Reemergence of Global Finance: From Bretton Woods to the 1990s*, Ithaca: Cornell University Press.

Kenen P. B. (1995), *Economic and Monetary Union in Europe: Moving beyond Maastricht*, England: Cambridge University Press.

Nowak A. Z. (2013), "Współczesny świat w erze turbulencji" (Contemporary World at the Time of Turbulence) in: *Zarządzanie: tradycja i nowoczesność* (*Management: Tradition and Modernity*), Bogdanienko J., Piotrowski W. (eds.), Warsaw: PWE.

Nowak A. Z., Shachmurove Y. (2012), "End of Euro Area?", in: *Understanding Global Economy – National and Regional Studies*, The Faculty of Management, Warsaw: University of Warsaw Press.

Nowak A. Z. (2012), "End of Euro Area?", in: *European Integrations Process in the New Regional and Global Settings*, Latoszek E., Kotowska I., A. Z. Nowak, Stępniak A. (eds.), The Faculty of Management, Warsaw: University of Warsaw Press.

Taplin R., Nowak A. Z. (2010), *Intellectual Property, Innovation and Management in Emerging Economies*, London: Routledge.

Tchorek G. (2011), *Teoretyczne podstawy integracji walutowej* (Theoretic Foudations of Monetary Integration), in: *Mechanizmy funkcjonowania strefy euro* (*Mechanisms of the Functioning Eurozone*), Kowalewski P., Tchorek G., Górski J. (eds.), Warsaw: NBP.

Ryć K., Nowak A.Z. (2010), "Euro Will Be Later – Costs or Benefits?", in: *Problemy nacjonalnoj strategii* (*Problems of National Strategy*), Moscow: Gosudarstwiennyj Institut Strategiczeskich Isliedowanii.

Wojtyna A. (2000), *Ewolucja keynesizmu a główny nurt ekonomii* (*The Evolution of Keynesianism and the Economy Mainstream*), Warsaw.

Other sources

Heller J., Kotliński K., "Trwała destabilizacja finansów publicznych a stopa bezrobocia w wybranych krajach Unii Europejskiej", *Studia Europejskie*, No. 4(64) 2012.

"Hollande retournera sur le site d'Arcelor Mittal à Florange le 23 septembre", *Le Monde*, 23 September 2013.

Lutkowski K., "Co się stało w strefie euro?" (What happened in Euro Area?), "Rzeczpospolita", 15 June 2012.

Kawalec S., Pytlarczyk E., Kontrolowana dekompozycja strefy euro, aby uratować Unię Europejską (Controlled decomposition of Euro Area – to Save the European Union), http://liberte.pl/ 27 June 2012.

Krugman, P. (2011, January), "Can Europe Be Saved?", *New York Times Magazine*. Report, World Economic Outlook, December 2012.

Rey H., "The Emergence of the Euro as an International Currency", in: Portes R., *Economic Policy*, 26 April 1998.

Regulation (EU) No. 1174/2011 of the European Parliament and of the Council of 16 November 2011 on enforcement measures to correct excessive macroeconomic imbalances in the euro area.

Alojzy Z. Nowak,
Kazimierz Ryć

Euro or Zloty?[1]

Introduction

The events taking place recently in Ukraine caused, among other things, renewed debate in Poland about the need for accession to the Euro Area as soon as possible. As noted by some economists, along with politicians and representatives of business circles, staying outside the Euro Area for any longer during the period of turbulence suffered in close geographic proximity to our borders may expose Poland to many disadvantages related, *inter alia*, with potential attacks of stock exchange speculators, or deterioration of assessments of situation in the region, with such possible effects as depreciation of Polish Zloty, etc.

Leaving aside, for the moment, the fact that at present neither the Euro Area nor Poland are ready for the enlargement of the Eurozone, the problem of Poland's accession to Euro Area is indeed important, both in theoretical and practical terms. Actually, it is also linked to the question whether it is an exogenous or an endogenous money – in relation to a country's economy – that better serves national economy over periods of financial or political turbulence and has a better influence upon business cycles. Although it is known that neither has Poland satisfied all the criteria essential for its accession to Euro Area yet, nor has the Economic and Monetary Union been really prepared at the moment to accommodate such a significant enlargement, considering how it still struggles with problems of fiscal crisis and structural reforms, still it is worthwhile and indeed necessary to address the subject of costs and benefits of Poland's accession to Euro Area, taking into account the vast pool of experience gathered over the recent crisis and the present slump.

The debate about Poland's accession to the Euro Area becomes heated in a cyclical manner. We saw this at the outset of the most recent financial crisis and we see the same thing now, as a result of social and political turbulence in Ukraine.

1 Nowak A. Z., Ryć K., "Złoty czy euro" (Zloty or Euro), *Rzeczpospolita*, 26 March 2014.

Poland – How Soon to the Euro Area?

There have been at least two attitudes stemming from opinions and arguments presented by the press, concerning Poland's accession to the Euro Area. One of them suggests that Poland should become a member of the EMU as soon as practicable, having first analysed all costs and benefits, of course. It seems safe to assess this attitude as rather emotional, provoked by recent political tension in Ukraine. Another position, on the other hand, advises to slow down the hurry-up attitude since it is far better at the present moment for Poland to remain outside Euro Area thus providing much more benefits than threats, in particular through the effect of maintaining a floating exchange rate of Polish Zloty. Namely, in the case of an unexpected decline of exports, depreciation of the Polish Zloty not only gives opportunities to maintain its volume but even makes it possible to increase production and therefore to raise an employment level.

Both above-mentioned positions, on the one hand, encourage us to reconsider the consequences of the introduction of Euro and, on the other hand, they make it clear that benefits and disadvantages of the Euro introduction should be assessed in both short- and long-term. It seems fundamental to answer the question what serves better the competitiveness of Polish economy and what enables the country to prepare better and avoid the so-called middle income country trap: is it membership in Euro Area or staying outside of it? This is not an easy question to answer. However, it may be plausibly argued that in the short term it may be of more advantage to stay outside the Euro Area and to maintain floating exchange rate for the currency for preservation or even improvement of Polish economic competitiveness. In case any economic turbulence should happen, and not only under such bleak scenarios, depreciation of the Polish Zloty reduces prices for foreign buyers and on a transitional basis this may even reduce manufacturing costs. In the long run, however – as Professor M. Belka rightly points out – this may lead to competitiveness being consolidated on the basis of low wages and extensive production technologies. Indeed the celebrated authority on economic competitiveness, Prof. Michael Porter has repeatedly asserted that neither driving down wages nor currency devaluations per se are source of genuine sustainable competitiveness. Thus this type of competition increases the likelihood of occurrence of the so-called middle-income limit because the above-mentioned competitiveness neither stems from real innovativeness nor from genuine entrepreneurship – instead, it is only a result of low labour costs. Also, manufacturers of such goods are not price leaders in the market, so their incomes are unlikely to be near the top levels – they are average at best. Also, a country that remains beyond a common currency zone is rarely leading in generation and export of branded goods.

In most cases, if involved in manufacturing of this type of goods at all, the country that retains a flexible rate remaining outside a common currency area rather tends to play the role of a subcontractor – a producer and exporter of parts or components thereof. Usually, it a company (an international corporation) having its seat in a common currency member state that acts as manufacturer of end products. This way such companies earn a sort of double income: once by employing cheaper production factors in a subcontractor country which provides them with components, and again by importing the same and paying less as a result of depreciation of Polish Zloty. If we calculate this in PLN, they earn more money on each item of the product, whereas in their own currency they have to pay less money. That's how they take advantage of the depreciation bonus. This may lead to relative impoverishment of a subcontractor's country or at least to freezing it into its status quo, known as the middle income limit.

It may be argued, therefore, that while the depreciation of the years 2008–2009, mentioned by Professor Belka in his interview, managed to make up, with a surplus, if calculated in terms of value in PLN, a slump in exports resulting from the crisis of 2007–2009, still the growth of exporters' income failed to translate into a correspondent growth of wages, levels of investment and employment. Extraordinary profits achieved, both on export by mother companies and by daughter companies in their mutual dealings, had the effect of generating income redistribution to the benefit of international corporations, all at the expense of domestic product. This served to further consolidate Poland's status as a cheap subcontractor, competing with low labour costs and occasionally earning Poland the epithet of *Europe's China*. At the same time, this sort of situation can lead to an increased threat of speculation by international investors. Encouraged by exorbitant profits made on depreciation of Polish zloty, they may assume short positions on Polish assets in order to buy the same at lower prices later on – namely, once the capital outflow they provoke results in Polish currency depreciation. In consequence, such manipulation may – under certain circumstances and in particular in a country featuring small open economy – even result in de facto loss of its monetary and currency sovereignty. In other words, in the extreme cases a country can be left with just a passive role with respect to the operations of what has been dubbed casino capitalism (See Chapter 1).

In the long run, therefore, in order to improve a country's competitiveness but also to avoid perturbations linked to speculative attacks against the currency of a small open market economy and in order to overcome the middle income level trap, it may be helpful to enter the common currency area. Possession of a common currency protects a country from manipulation of its exchange rates with a view to achieving short-term benefits and better immunises its market against all sorts of currency-related speculation. It may also be assume, hypothetically at least since Poland hasn't had an opportunity to experience this, that in the short run membership in Euro Area, in particular in the aftermath and consequences of the 2008 crisis, would also probably have meant smaller outflow of foreign capital and lower growth of debt servicing costs, in terms of both public and private indebtedness, and especially of debt related with credits in foreign currencies. At the same time, one could also expect negative consequences, such as likely economic overheating due to the effect of low interest rates as happened in other, less developed Euro Area countries or in those applying currency board regime and the inevitable cyclical downturn and slow-down of growth that follows the period of overheating.

It should also be borne in mind what the case of Greece, Spain, Portugal and Ireland teaches: namely, that in a Euro Area relying upon the common currency and in policy terms only on a common monetary policy mainly oriented at the achievement of an inflation target, this may also lead to various types of divergences and degenerations the consequences of which may end up being extremely painful to individual economies.

Endogenous and Exogenous Currency

Accession to the Euro Area implies that the nature of the currency changes from endogenous to exogenous; in other words, sovereign monetary policy has to be given up by the nation state, although in any small open economy that sovereignty is very limited even before that. In the case of Poland the Euro would become such an exogenous currency. This is a qualitative change capable of having a very significant impact upon the economy and on the principles of functioning of every group member.

While in the theory behind Robert Mundell's optimum currency area the currency under that system wasn't actually meant to be exogenous in the Euro Area it has become so. Mundell assumed that through high flexibility of production factors, i.e. free movement of both labour and capital on the one hand, and on the other hand due to potential redistribution of fiscal revenues in order to support regions experiencing failures on the other hand, the economy of the entire optimum currency area would operate under conditions similar to an economy of a single country, so that the common currency would really be endogenous in nature, enabling a uniform monetary policy to be run for the entire area. In reality things did not happen this way in the monetary union – or at least not completely.

The problem of the Euro's exogenous nature was already present in the background when the bodies behind establishment of the Economic and Monetary Union decided to create the optimum currency area, reckoning *ex ante* that the common currency would accelerate the process of real convergence with parallel improvement of freedom of market mechanisms, released from exchange rate-related risk and from transaction costs. Again, things did not happen this way, as fully revealed by the crisis of 2008 and painful adaptation problems faced in many European Union member states in its wake.

As a matter of fact, we largely have to deal with exogenous currency in the Euro Area, although at present the ECB keeps moving in, actually or just verbally, in favour of individual countries, with the result that the Euro sometimes alters its nature into an incidentally endogenous currency, thus making it easier to go through the adaptation process to a single currency at least in some countries (for example, a promise of government bond buying up by the ECB).

All in all, however, the hitherto-existing currency in the Euro Area has remained exogenous with respect to all the Euro Area member states – a fact which has made it harder rather than any easier to proceed with harmonious growth of the area, in virtually all aspects of real convergence.

Meanwhile, it seems that in face of such a great economic diversity as exists among Euro Area member states, the common currency should, ideally at least, have a partially endogenous nature, which would enable their economies to adapt to requirements posed by business cycle conditions. This is especially important when currency integration is really only based upon currency and monetary policy only focused upon the inflation target.

As a result of, among other things, non-endogenous nature of the currency, the Euro Area has seen gradual emergence of the so-called "friendly states," the peculiarity of which has been over long periods, government spending well in excess of their revenues. What has resulted is a lack of convergence in development of individual countries as well as difficulties in achieving, for example, the priority of external over internal balance.

Conclusions

As is evident, even based on such a concise analysis, it is not from every point of view that the Euro Area in its hitherto-existing form may be unambiguously favourably assessed. Nevertheless, the effects of its operation as well as the experience collected as a result of the global financial crisis and, even more so, the lack of better alternatives, suggest it is worthwhile for Poland to seriously consider relatively prompt accession thereto.

However, one should also take into account that exogenous currencies seem to perform rather worse in democratic than in an elitist or authoritarian society. This may be concluded based on historical experience with commodity money and previous monetary unions. Such exogenous currencies perform well over periods of tranquillity but fail at the time of shocks and crises when the need for external adaptations prevails over an economy's internal adaptations. In such cases state social expenditure falls foul of the imposed savings, necessary for reconstruction of external balance, while real incomes of less wealthy parts of society decrease. Tightening belts gives rise to social tensions and dissatisfaction of the electorate. Under such circumstances endogenous currency would make it possible to overcome such a difficult period of adaptation in a smoother manner, although not necessarily at lower costs. Actually, costs might even be higher, while hidden in financial machinations, non-transparent processes of income redistribution, phenomena of inflation, etc. spread over time but which in the final analysis are not less burdensome for the society.

The problem is how to retain the common currency of Euro and still to give it some attributes of endogenous currency during the process of reform. This is about possibilities to react for the ECB and then for the banking system over periods of threats, and in a selective manner, for the needs of only some member states. If the Banking Union is able to satisfy this sort of expectation as well, then it will relieve or even eliminate some negative properties of exogenous currency.

Another unexpected lever, which could alleviate the processes of adaptation and real convergence of the monetary union member states, would be sector-specific policy or new industrial policy. It is our hope that the concept, recently promoted by Brussels, of intelligent specialisation of regions and countries, and of more vertical economic policy, is also going to facilitate the process of real convergence and integration. In Poland, we should monitor these evolutions with much diligence and support them as far as we reasonably can.

In our opinion the common currency has a future and is here to stay; therefore, Poland, considered as a small open economy trading extensively with the rest of the EU, should accede thereto. This is why we believe that Poland should be actively taking steps to promote accession to a renewed Monetary Union. However, Poland certainly should not nervously rush into hastily becoming a member.

Bibliography

Belka M., "Wyczynowy kapitalizm do poprawki" (High-Performance Capitalism Due for Corrections), *Dziennik Gazeta Prawna*, 14 February 2014.

Nowak A. Z., Ryć K., "Europa potrzebuje liberalnego Keynesa?" (Europe Needs A Liberal Keynes?), *Rzeczpospolita*, 26 November 2013.

Nowak A. Z., Ryć K., "Złoty czy euro" (Zloty or Euro), *Rzeczpospolita*, 26 March 2014.

Mundell R. A., "A Theory of Optimum Currency Areas", in: *The American Economic Review* 51 (4), September 1961.

Wojtyna A., "Ukraina a euro w Polsce" (Ukraine and Euro in Poland), *Rzeczpospolita*, 5 March 2014.

Studies in Politics, Security and Society

Edited by Stanisław Sulowski

Vol. 1 Robert Wiszniowski (ed.): Challenges to Representative Democracy. A European Perspective. 2015.

Vol. 2 Jarosław Szymanek: Theory of Political Representation. 2015.

Vol. 3 Alojzy Z. Nowak (ed.): Global Financial Turbulence in the Euro Area. Polish Perspective. 2015.

Vol. 4 Jolanta Itrich-Drabarek: The Civil Service in Poland. Theory and Experience. 2015.

www.peterlang.com

www.ingramcontent.com/pod-product-compliance
Ingram Content Group UK Ltd.
Pitfield, Milton Keynes, MK11 3LW, UK
UKHW041827031026
15587UKWH00002B/606

9 783631 665657